Copyright © 2021 by Jordan C. Groh -All rights reserved.

No part of this publication may be reproduced, distributed, or transmitted in any form or by any means, including photocopying, recording, or other electronic or mechanical methods, without the prior written permission of the publisher, except in the case of brief quotations embodied in reviews and certain other non-commercial uses permitted by copyright law.

This Book is provided with the sole purpose of providing relevant information on a specific topic for which every reasonable effort has been made to ensure that it is both accurate and reasonable. Nevertheless, by purchasing this Book you consent to the fact that the author, as well as the publisher, are in no way experts on the topics contained herein, regardless of any claims as such that may be made within. It is recommended that you always consult a professional prior to undertaking any of the advice or techniques discussed within.This is a legally binding declaration that is considered both valid and fair by both the Committee of Publishers Association and the American Bar Association and should be considered as legally binding within the United States.

CONTENTS

INTRODUCTION 6
CHAPTER 1: WHAT IS NINJA FOODI FRYER? 6
    Benefits of Ninja Air Fryer 6
    Common operation buttons 7
    Tips for Using the Ninja Foodi 8
CHAPTER 2: BREAKFAST RECIPES 10
    Veggie Hash Brown 10
    Sicilian Cauliflower Roast Crunch 10
    Heartfelt Spinach Quiche 11
    Breakfast Broccoli Casserole 11
    Creamy Asparagus Soup 12
    Amazing Bacon and Veggie Delight 13
    Hearty Broccoli and Scrambled Cheese Breakfast 13
    Original Onion and Scrambled Tofu 14
    Ballet of Ham and Spinach 14
    Egg Broccoli Quiche 15
    Kale Sausage Breakfast 16
    Coconut Breakfast Bagels 16
    Pineapple French Toast 17
    Creamed French Toast 17
    Cheesy Egg Bites 18
    Everyday Poached Eggs 19
    Low-Carb Blueberry Muffins 19
    Veggie Frittata 20
    Breakfast Casserole 21
    Crustless Sausage and Mushroom Quiche 22
    Mexican Breakfast Bowls 22
    Giant Pancake 23
    Morning Hashes 24
    Scrambled Cheese Eggs with Broccoli 24
    Spinach Quiche 25
    Mushroom Tofu 26
    Bacon and Veggies 26
    Scrambled Onion Tofu 26
    Omelet with Pepperoni 27
    Bok Choy Samba with Bacon 27
CHAPTER 3: POULTRY RECIPES 29
    Chicken 29
        Hot Chicken Wings 29
        Basil & Cheddar Stuffed Chicken 29
        Honey-Glazed Chicken Kabobs 30
        Chicken with Prunes 30
        Chicken Burgers with Avocado 31
        Crunchy Chicken Schnitzels 31
        Cordon Bleu Chicken 32
        Rosemary Lemon Chicken 33
        Greek-Style Chicken 33
        Asian-Style Chicken 34
        Crumbed Sage Chicken Scallopini 34
        Chicken Tenders with Broccoli & Rice 35
        Buttermilk Chicken Thighs 36
        Roasted Crisp Whole Chicken 36
        Ginger-Balsamic Glazed Chicken 37
        Tasty Sesame-Honeyed Chicken 37

- Traditional Chicken 'n Dumplings 38
- Garlic Chicken in Creamy Tuscan Style 39
- Green Curry Chicken Thai Style 39
- Savory 'n Aromatic Chicken Adobo 40
- Duck 40
- Duck with Asparagus 41
- Parsley Duck and Fennel 41
- Duck with Berries Mix 41
- Garlic Duck and Apples 42
- Thyme Duck 42
- Turkey 43
  - Hot Turkey Cutlets 43
  - Turkey Potato Pie 44
  - Turkey Dinner Risotto 44
  - Italian Turkey Roast 45
  - Funky-Garlic And turkey Breasts 46

CHAPTER 4: FISH RECIPES 47
- Salmon Stew 47
- Paprika Shrimp 47
- Butter Fish 48
- Delicious Shrimps 48
- Sweet and Sour Fish 48
- Buttery Scallops 49
- Cod with Herbs 49
- Glazed Salmon 50
- Cajun Salmon 51
- Spicy Fried Salmon with Avocado Salsa 51
- Shrimp Bisque 52
- Fried Scallops in Cilantro Sauce 52
- Breaded Trout with Parsley Pesto 53
- Paprika Tuna Cakes 54
- Red Wine Poached Salmon 55
- Garlic Lemon Shrimp with Asparagus 55
- Tuna in Mango Sauce 56
- Cod Topped with Mediterranean-Spiced Tomatoes 57
- Tilapia Filet Topped with Mango-Salsa 57
- Coconut Curry Sea Bass 58
- Tomato-Basil Dressed Tilapia 59
- Pasta 'n Tuna Bake 59
- Salmon-Pesto Over Pasta 60
- Sweet 'n Spicy Mahi-Mahi 61
- Easy Veggie-Salmon Bake 61
- Salmon with Orange-Ginger Sauce 62
- Coconut Curry Fish 63
- Seafood Gumbo New Orleans Style 63
- Creamy Herb 'n Parm Salmon 64
- Stewed Mixed Seafood 65

CHAPTER 5: BEEF RECIPES 66
- Beef 'n Mushrooms in Thick Sauce 66
- Beef Stew Recipe from Ethiopia 66
- Beef Cooked in Mango-Turmeric Spice 67
- St. Patty's Corned Beef Recipe 68
- Potatoes, Beefy-Cheesy Way 68
- Beef Pot Pie 69
- Healthy 'n Tasty Meatloaf 70
- Beefy Stew Recipe from Persia 70
- Bacon-Wrapped Hot Dogs 71

Wholesome Asparagus Beef	72
Warm and Beefy Meat Loaf	72
Wise Corned Beef	73
Elegant Beef Curry	74
Mesmerizing Beef Sirloin Steak	74
Epic Beef Sausage Soup	75
The Indian Beef Delight	75
Fresh Korean Braised Ribs	76
The Classical Corned Beef and Cabbage	77
The Ultimate One-Pot Beef Roast	77
Easy to Swallow Beef Ribs	78
The Gentle Beef and Broccoli Dish	79
The Juicy Beef Chili	79
Generous Ground Beef Stew	80
Spiced Beef Shapes	81
Thai Roasted Beef	81
Peppercorn Meatloaf	82
Beef Congee with Kale	83
Beef Pasta Mania	83
Beef Meatballs in Honey-Orange Sauce	84
Spicy Beef Pitas	85

CHAPTER 6: PORK 30 RECIPES **87**

Broccoli Pork with Rice	87
Tangy Pork Carnitas	87
Bourbon Pork Chops	88
Classic Pork Meal with Green Bean	89
Southern-Style Lettuce Wraps	90
Orecchiette and Pork Ragu	90
Mustard Dredged Pork Chops	91
Authentic Beginner Friendly Pork Belly	91
Deliciously Spicy Pork Salad Bowl	92
Special "Swiss" Pork chops	93
Perfect Sichuan Pork Soup	93
Healthy Cranberry BBQ Pork	94
Decisive Kalua Pork	95
Easy-Going Kid Friendly Pork Chops	95
Amazing Mexican Pulled Pork Lettuce	96
Bacon Pork Chops	97
Jamaican Jerk Pork Roast	97
Pork Carnitas	98
Mustard Pork Chops	98
Spicy Pork Ribs	99
Pork Chops with Cabbage	99
BBQ Pork Chops	100
Seasoned Pork Tenderloin	100
Spicy Pork Loin	101
Shredded Pork Shoulder	102
Apple and Onion Topped Pork Chops	102
The Crispiest Roast Pork	103
Philippine-Style Pork Chops	103
Honey Barbecue Pork Ribs	104
Char Siew Pork Ribs	105

CHAPTER 7: VEGETABLES 20 RECIPES **106**

Chives Beets and Carrots	106
Minty Radishes	106
Carrots and Walnuts Salad	106
Soy Kale	107

Chili Eggplant and Kale	107
Lime Broccoli and Cauliflower	108
Garlic Red Bell Peppers Mix	108
Zucchinis and Spinach Mix	109
Potatoes and Lemon Sauce	110
Lemony Leeks and Carrots	110
Sesame Radish and Leeks	110
Radish and Apples Mix	111
Lime Cabbage and Bacon	111
Napa Cabbage and Carrots	112
Parsley Kale and Leeks	112
Balsamic Cabbage and Endives	113
Creamy Kale	113
Kale and Parmesan	114
Pomegranate Radish Mix	115
Pine Nuts Okra and Leeks	115

CHAPTER 8: DESSERTS & APPETIZERS 20 RECIPES 116

Tapioca Pudding	116
New York Style Cheesecake	116
Yellow Cake Pineapple Upside Down	117
Raspberry Cheesecake	117
Caramel Popcorns	118
Chocolate Crème de Pot	119
Apricots Dulche de Leche	120
Blackberry Cobbler	120
Mango Rice Pudding	121
Baked Stuffed Apples	121
Sugar Cookie Pizza	122
Sweet and Salty Bars	122
Coconut Rice Pudding	123
Cheese Babka	124
Coconut Cream "Custard" Bars	125
Apple Crisp	126
Brownie Bites	126
Bacon Blondies	127
Peanut Butter Pie	128
Chocolate Peanut Butter and Jelly Puffs	128

CHAPTER 9: DRINKS 10 RECIPES 130

Nut Porridge	130
Deliciously Traditional Clam Chowder	130
Vanilla Yogurt	131
White Cream Soup	131
Good-Day Pumpkin Puree	132
Sweet Potato 'n Garbanzo Soup	132
Vanilla Pudding with Berries	133
Apple Pie Moonshine	133
Chili-Quinoa 'n Black Bean Soup	134
Filling Cauli-Squash Chowder	135

INTRODUCTION

I want to thank you and congratulate you for downloading this book. Cooking your own food has a lot of advantages and one of them is that you can be certain of its nutritional profile because you know what goes into your food. And while cooking your own meals is the best way to be healthy, there are still so many people who are tempted to go back to their usual unhealthy eating habits because it is more convenient than slaving all day in the kitchen.

The Ninja Foodi comes to help you cook any type of food from fries, steak, to desserts, all in one appliance. This kitchen appliance saves you money as you do not have buy in many other kitchen gadgets because it is a multicooker. You can cook any meal you want easily.

This book has information about this great kitchen appliance and many recipes that can be cooked using it. The recipes are put into categories to make it easier for you. Read on to know more.

Thanks for downloading this book. Enjoy reading!

CHAPTER 1: WHAT IS NINJA FOODI FRYER?

The Ninja Foodi is a multipurpose, user-friendly kitchen appliance that you could have. It's a sauté pan, air fryer, electric pressure cooker, rice cooker and slow cooker all in one.

This air fryer and pressure cooker combination cooks food faster and more efficiently than any other kitchen appliance. It can be used to cook a variety of meals like stews, chicken soup, classic roast etc.

How it works

The Ninja Foodi may have the most functions among many multicookers sold in the market but it does not mean that it is very difficult to operate. Contrary to popular belief, it is one of the easiest multicooker to operate despite of its bulk and complexity in design (because of the presence of the crisping and pressure lid). This section will enlighten you on how you can use and optimize your Ninja Foodi.

Benefits of Ninja Air Fryer

Fast cooking: It greatly decreases typically long cooking times for all dishes. Cooking time can be reduced 60% to 80% (depending on the ingredient). Faster cooking times mean you can cook real foods from scratch in the time it takes for pizza delivery or to prepare a frozen dinner.

Safe and user-friendly: Ninja Foodi is pre-programmed, and therefore, incidents such as exploding of the cooker do not happen. It has features which are pre-programmed and therefore, all you have to do is to press the correct cooking button.

Saves Energy: It cooks food faster thus reducing cooking significantly. Reduced cooking time translates to energy saving. It can be the only appliance you use therefore making it economical.

Maintaining Nutritional Value: As opposed to most of the existing cooking methods which drain or destroy food's nutrition, the Ninja Air Fryer preserves the nutritional value of the foods being cooked.

It is Convenient: No longer do you have to bother about the size of your kitchen or where you will store the multitude of kitchen appliances needed to concoct one single home cooked meals. Simply place all of your ingredients in your Ninja Air Fryer and allow it do its thing automatically.

Common operation buttons

The control panel of the Ninja Foodi comes with a few operation buttons that allow you to control different cooking factors on the multicooker. Below is a discussion of the basic operation buttons found on Ninja Foodi's control panel.

- **Power**: this button allows you to turn off and shut off the unit and stop the active cooking function.
- **Pre-set cooking button:** there are more pre-set cooking buttons found on Ninja Foodi than other multicookers in the market. These pre-set cooking buttons include (1) pressure, (2) steam, (3) sear/sauté, (4) slow cook, (5) bake/roast, (6) air crisp, (7) dehydrate, and (8) broil. For more information on how these pre-set cooking buttons work, it will be discussed in the next section.
- **Temp arrows**: this button allows you to adjust the cooking temperature including the pressure. Use the arrow up to increase the setting and arrow down to decrease it.
- **Time arrows:** this allows you to adjust the cooking time. Use the arrow up to increase cooking time and the arrow down to do the opposite.
- **Start/stop button:** pressing this button will star the multicooker to cook your food. Pressing it again while it is in operation will stop the cooking process.
- **Keep warm:** this button keeps your food warm at safe temperature. You can opt for this function after slow cooking, pressure cooking, and steaming. Once you press this button, it will automatically start counting up until you press the stop button.
- **Standby:** ten (10) minutes without any interaction with the control panel, this function will immediately activate. However, it will only activate once the power and start buttons have been pressed.

Pre-set cooking buttons

The pre-set cooking buttons allow you to cook foods without the guesswork thus you can cook even the most complicated food even if you are a novice. With the preset cooking button, the Ninja Foodi will be the one to cook the food based on the setting you have chosen using pre-programmed temperature and circulation so that you can cook food depending on the setting that you have chosen. When cooking food using the Ninja Foodi, it is important that you become familiar with the pre-set cooking buttons work.

Pressure: this allows you to cook food through pressure cooking. With this pre-set cooking button, it allows you to cook food 70% faster compared to conventional methods.

Slow cook: this pre-set cooking button allows you to cook food at low temperature similar with a slow cooker. Use the pressure lid but do not set the vent to sealed. You can adjust the cooking time between 4 and 12 hours depending on the type of food that you are cooking. The keep warm function will turn on once the cooking time is complete.

Steam: steam your food gently at high temperature. Use at least one cup of liquid to steam your food and use the accompanying rack. Use the pressure lid and set the vent to seal for this function.

Air crisp: this allows you to transform the multicooker into a Ninja Foodi. This setting cooks the food between 3000f and 4000f. Make sure to preheat the ninja food first for at least five minutes before adding the ingredients. Use the crisping lid for this pre-set cooking button.

Sear/sauté: turn your Ninja Foodi into a sear buttoning pan with this function. It is good in sear buttoning meat, sautéing, or toasting spices. Do not use any lid with this pre-set button. You can also use it to simmer or thicken sauces. You can use the lid for simmering but make sure that it is not sealed in place. This pre-set cooking button does not come with a time adjustment so just press the start/stop button if you want to start or stop this function.

Broil: this pre-set cooking button allows you to caramelize or sear button the surface of your food. Use the crisping lid with this function. There is no temperature adjustment for this pre-set cooking button, but you can adjust the cooking time depending on what you are cooking. And just like the air crisper, preheat the unit first before adding the ingredients.

Bake/roast: this setting converts the multicooker into an oven. This allows you to cook food between 2000F and 4000F.use the crisping lid to roast meats, veggies, or make baked goodies. Make sure to preheat the unit first before putting in the food.

Dehydrate: this pre-set cooking button allows you to dehydrate different kinds of ingredients so that you can make healthy snacks. Dehydrate foods from 105°F to 195°F. We recommend that you get the dehydrating rack, so you have more area to dehydrate your food.

Tips for Using the Ninja Foodi

With 14 multiple layers of safety, Ninja Foodi allows cooking to cook without worrying about their safety in any manner. But you can further boost your confidence by following a few tips before beginning your cooking experience with Ninja Foodi.

Here are all those tips you should use when using Ninja Foodi as a newbie:

Understand every function

Ninja Foodi is a multicooker, which comes with various cooking functionalities. You have already read about the functions of pressure cooking, air frying, steaming, searing, sautéing, baking, crisping, and others. Other functions include Tender Crisp, steaming, and others.

To effectively utilize this appliance, it would be wise to understand every function and its benefit before moving forward. Using this knowledge of functionality, you can choose your dishes wisely and cook more efficiently.

Pick simple dishes in the beginning

The diversity of cooking styles in Ninja Foodi can seem overwhelming to newbies. So, it is better to relax and cook simple dishes initially.

You can start with simple one-pot stews and soups to make yourself comfortable with the control panel and functions of the pot.

Eventually, you will find yourself remembering the process and utilizing each and every function of the pot. Then, you can move toward more complex food options and cook multi-combination meals in one go.

Go through the manual instructions
This pot comes with simple and understandable manual instructions. So, that should not be a problem. Just make sure you don't jump right into using the pot without reading the manual. Give a few minutes before you are ready to cook your very first meal.

Practice as frequently as possible
Cooking once or twice a week won't help if you are a newbie at pressure cooking. You need to frequently cook dishes as many times as possible. The more you cook the better you will get at using all the functions.

Ninja Foodi saves from wasting time in thawing a frozen food. So, you can simply transfer a food straight from the refrigerator to the pot. The air fryer technology works with pressure cooking to make your food tender and crispy. Plus, your food keeps the juices intact.

By this way, you can cook more in lesser time and enjoy delicious chicken, pork, beef, and other food items. But it all comes down to how many times you cook initially to make yourself more and more competent with the functions of the pot.

Try a new dish every day
To improve your cooking capabilities, you need to go beyond your comfort zone every day. Of course, you start with simple dishes in the beginning, but don't get stuck in those same dishes. Cooking is fun when you try new dishes every day. And thanks to Ninja Foodi, you will have all the functions available in one pot to cook different desserts, vegetables, poultry, fish, and red meat recipes.

Utilize attached accessories
Along with a nonstick cooking pot, Ninja Foodi comes with other attached accessories such as a crisping lid, a basket, a reversible rack, and a pressure lid as well. Every accessory serves a purpose. From sealing the pot to frying it internally, every cooking advantage is possible only when you use all the attached accessories efficiently.

CHAPTER 2: BREAKFAST RECIPES

Veggie Hash Brown

This great recipe is an awesome way to start your day. It gives you the much-needed energy and nutrients to jumpstart your day. It is also very easy to prepare.

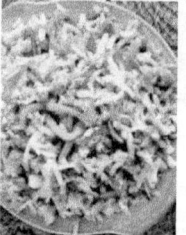

Prep time 10 minutes/ Cook time 20 minutes/ Serves 4

Ingredients:
- 1 tablespoon unsalted butter
- ½ teaspoon dried thyme, crushed
- ½ cup cauliflower florets, boiled, chopped
- ½ small onion, chopped
- ½ cup water
- Salt and pepper to taste
- ½ pound turkey meat, chopped
- ¼ cup heavy cream

Directions
1. Set your Ninja Foodi to Sauté mode and let it heat up, add butter and let the butter melt
2. Add onion and Sauté for 3 minutes
3. Add chopped cauliflowers
4. Saute for 2 minutes longer
5. Add turkey and water
6. Close Pressure lid and set your Ninja Foodi to HIGH pressure mode, cook for 10 minutes
7. Quick release the pressure
8. Set the Ninja Foodie to BROIL mode (lid open) and add heavy cream, close the lid and let it Broil for 2 minutes
9. Serve and enjoy!

Per Serving: Calories 151, Carbs 0.7 g, Fats 11 g, Protein 11 g

Sicilian Cauliflower Roast Crunch

This is a straight forward and easy dish for anyone to try out, and with the Ninja Foodi, you are more likely to make it successfully, even if it is your first time.

Prep time 10 minutes/ Cook time 10 minutes/ Serves 4

Ingredients
- 1 medium cauliflower head, leaves removed
- ¼ cup olive oil
- 1 teaspoon red pepper, crushed
- ½ cup water
- 2 tablespoons capers, rinsed, minced
- ½ cup parmesan cheese, grated

- 1 tablespoon fresh parsley, chopped

Directions
1. Prepare the Ninja Foodi by adding water and place the cook and crisp basket inside the pot
2. Cut an "X" on the head of cauliflower by using a knife and slice it about halfway down
3. Take a basket and transfer the cauliflower in it
4. Then put on the pressure lid and seal it and set it on low pressure for 3 minutes
5. Add olive oil, capers, garlic, and crushed red pepper into it and mix them well
6. Once the cauliflower is cooked, do a quick release and remove the lid
7. Pour in the oil and spice mixture on the cauliflower
8. Spread equally on the surface then sprinkle some Parmesan cheese from the top
9. Close the pot with crisping lid
10. Set it on Air Crisp mode to 390 degrees F for 10 minutes
11. Once done, remove the cauliflower flower the Ninja Foodi transfer it into a serving plate
12. Cut it up into pieces and transfer them to serving plates
13. Sprinkle fresh parsley from the top
14. Serve and enjoy!

Per Serving: Calories 119, Carbs 5 g, Protein 2.2 g, Fats 10 g

Heartfelt Spinach Quiche

It is important that you start your day with an amazing meal that would fuel you for the rest of the day, and this meal is just that.

Prep time 10 minutes/ Cook time 33 minutes/ Serves 4

Ingredients
- 1 tablespoon butter, melted
- 1 pack frozen spinach, thawed
- 5 organic eggs, beaten
- Salt and pepper to taste
- 3 cups Monterey Jack Cheese, shredded

Directions
1. Set your Ninja Foodi to Saute mode and let it heat up, add butter and let the butter melt
2. Add spinach and Saute for 3 minutes, transfer the Sautéed spinach to a bowl
3. Add eggs, cheese, salt and pepper to a bowl and mix it well
4. Transfer the mixture to greased quiche molds and transfer the mold to your Foodi
5. Close lid and choose the "Bake/Roast" mode and let it cook for 30 minutes at 360 degrees F
6. Once done, open lid and transfer the dish out
7. Cut into wedges and serve

Per Serving: Calories 349, Carbs 3.2 g. Fats 27 g, Protein 23 g

Breakfast Broccoli Casserole

Are you looking for a perfect casserole to serve for breakfast? The Broccoli casserole is a perfect dish for breakfast, it also fits perfectly for brunch. It comes out great in the Ninja Foodi, and you will enjoy making it with your appliance.

Prep time 10 minutes/ Cook time 7 minutes/ Serves 4

Ingredients

- 1 tablespoon extra-virgin olive oil
- 1-pound broccoli, cut into florets
- 1-pound cauliflower, cut into florets
- ¼ cup almond flour
- 2 cups coconut milk
- ½ teaspoon ground nutmeg
- Pinch of pepper
- 1 and ½ cup shredded Gouda cheese, divided

Directions

1. Pre-heat your Ninja Foodi by setting it to Saute mode
2. Add olive oil and let it heat up, add broccoli and cauliflower
3. Take a medium bowl stir in almond flour, coconut milk, nutmeg, pepper, 1 cup cheese and add the mixture to your Ninja Foodi
4. Top with ½ cup cheese and lock lid, cook on HIGH pressure for 5 minutes
5. Release pressure naturally over 10 minutes
6. Serve and enjoy!

Per Serving: Calories 373, Fats 32 g, Carbs 6 g, Protein 16 g

Creamy Asparagus Soup

The best thing you can probably have on a cold day is a plate of fresh Creamy Asparagus Soup. It will make you feel good and wanting more. It is a dish that is very easy to make, and it takes very little time to prepare.

Prep time 10 minutes/ Cook time 10 minutes/ Serves 4

Ingredients

- 1 tablespoon olive oil
- 3 green onions, sliced crosswise into ¼ inch pieces
- 1-pound asparagus, tough ends removed, cut into 1-inch pieces
- 4 cups vegetable stock
- 1 tablespoon unsalted butter
- 1 tablespoon almond flour
- 2 teaspoon salt
- 1 teaspoon white pepper
- ½ cup heavy cream

Directions

1. Set your Ninja Foodi to "Saute" mode and add oil, let it heat up
2. Add green onions and Saute for a few minutes, add asparagus and stock
3. Lock lid and cook on high pressure for 5 minutes

4. Take a small saucepan and place it over low heat, add butter, flour and stir until the mixture foams and turns into a golden beige, this is your blond roux
5. Remove from heat
6. Release pressure naturally over 10 minutes
7. Open lid and add roux, salt and pepper to the soup
8. Use an immersion blender to puree the soup
9. Taste and season accordingly, swirl in cream and enjoy!

Per Serving: Calories 192, Carbs 8 g, Fats 14 g, Protein 6 g

Amazing Bacon and Veggie Delight

The most interesting thing about it is that it very easy to make, how good does that sound? While a lot of people will have to get their Instant Pot and their air fryer ready to make this, all you have to get ready is just your Ninja Foodi, and get ready to have a Ninja'd Bacon and Veggie Delight.

Prep time 5 minutes/ Cook time 25 minutes/ Serves 4

Ingredients
- 1 green bell pepper, chopped
- 4 bacon slices
- ½ cup parmesan cheese
- 1 tablespoon avocado mayonnaise
- 2 scallions, chopped

Directions
1. Arrange your bacon slices in your Ninja Foodi pot and top them up with avocado mayo, scallions, bell peppers, parmesan cheese
2. Close lid and select the Bake/Roast mode, set timer to 25 minutes and temperature to 365 degrees F
3. Let it bake and remove the dish after 25 minutes
4. Serve and enjoy!

Per Serving: Calories 197, Carbs 5 g, Protein 14 g, Fats 13 g

Hearty Broccoli and Scrambled Cheese Breakfast

This is a refreshing breakfast dish that will fill you and leave you wanting more. It is a very easy to make dish that will make your work in the kitchen very easy.

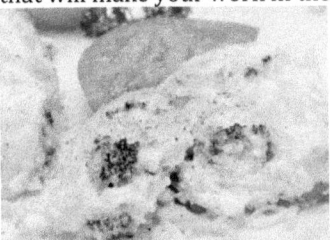

Prep time 10 minutes/ Cook time 5 minutes/ Serves 4

Ingredients
- 1 pack, 12 ounces frozen broccoli florets
- 2 tablespoons butter
- salt and pepper
- 8 whole eggs
- 2 tablespoons milk
- ¾ cup white cheddar cheese, shredded

- Crushed red pepper

Directions
1. Add butter and broccoli to your Ninja Foodi
2. Season with salt and pepper according to your taste
3. Set the Ninja to Medium Pressure mode and let it cook for about 10 minutes, covered, making sure to keep stirring the broccoli from time to time
4. Take a medium sized bowl and add crack in the eggs, beat the eggs gently
5. Pour milk into the eggs and give it a nice stir
6. Add the egg mixture into the Ninja (over broccoli) and gently stir, cook for 2 minutes (uncovered)
7. Once the egg has settled in, add cheese and sprinkle red pepper, black pepper, and salt
8. Enjoy with bacon strips if you prefer!

Per Serving: Calories 184, Carbs 5 g, Protein 12 g, Fats 12 g

Original Onion and Scrambled Tofu

This recipe is very crunchy and delicious. I can assure you it is something you can never get over and it is very easy to make.

Prep time 8 minutes/ Cook time 12 minutes/ Serves 4

Ingredients
- 4 tablespoons butter
- 2 tofu blocks, pressed and cubed in to 1-inch pieces
- Salt and pepper to taste
- 1 cup cheddar cheese, grated
- 2 medium onions, sliced

Directions
1. Take a bowl and add tofu, season with salt and pepper
2. Set your Foodi to Saute mode and add butter, let it melt
3. Add onions and Saute for 3 minutes
4. Add seasoned tofu and cook for 2 minutes more
5. Add cheddar and gently stir
6. Lock the lid and bring down the Air Crisp mode, let the dish cook on "Air Crisp" mode for 3 minutes at 340 degrees F
7. Once done, take the dish out, serve and enjoy!

Per Serving: Calories 184, Carbs 5 g, Fats 12 g, Protein 12 g

Ballet of Ham and Spinach

The way it sounds may make it seem difficult or stressful to coo, let this not scare you, it is the direct opposite of that. Even for very difficult recipes, I think, there are always ways to make it simpler and easier.

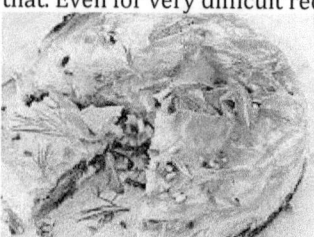

Prep time 5 minutes/ Cook time 30 minutes/ Serves 6

Ingredients
- 3 pounds fresh baby spinach

- ½ cup cream
- 28 ounces ham, sliced
- 4 tablespoons butter, melted
- Salt and pepper to taste

Directions
1. Set your Ninja Foodi to Saute mode and add butter, let it melt
2. Add spinach and Saute for 3 minutes
3. Top with cream, ham slices, salt and pepper
4. Lock the Air Fryer lid and let it Bake/Roast for 8 minutes at 360 degrees F
5. Remove the dish from the Foodi and serve
6. Enjoy!

Per Serving: Calories 188, Carbs 5 g, Protein 14 g, Fats 12 g

Egg Broccoli Quiche

This recipe is one of the easiest to make. It takes about 25 minutes to completely cook, it takes about 10 minutes of preparation time, and about 20 minutes of cooking time.

Prep time 10 minutes/ Cook time 20 minutes/ Serves 6

Ingredients
- 8 medium eggs
- ½ cup milk
- 1 cup Cheddar cheese, shredded
- 1 tablespoon extra-virgin olive oil
- 1 teaspoon sea salt
- 1 teaspoon ground black pepper
- 2 garlic cloves, minced
- 1 yellow onion, chopped
- 2 cups broccoli florets, thinly sliced
- 1 piecrust, at room temperature

Directions
1. In a mixing bowl, whisk the eggs; add the milk, salt, and pepper. Add the Cheddar cheese and whisk well.
2. Take Ninja Foodi multi-cooker, arrange it over a cooking platform, and open the top lid.
3. In the pot, add the oil; Select the "sear/sauté" mode and select the "HI" pressure level.
4. Press "stop/start." After about 4-5 minutes, the oil will start simmering.
5. Add the onions, garlic, and cook (while stirring) for 4-5 minutes until they become softened and translucent.
6. Add the broccoli; sauté for another 5 minutes.
7. Add the egg mixture over and gently stir-cook for 1 minute until the eggs cook well and incorporate.
8. In the pie crust, add the mixture. And fold the edges. For heat escape, make a small cut in the center of the piecrust.
9. Seal the multi-cooker by locking it with the crisping lid; ensure to keep the pressure release valve locked/sealed.
10. Select "broil" mode and select the "HI" pressure level. Then, set timer to 10 minutes and press "stop/start"; it will start the cooking process by building up inside pressure.
11. When the timer goes off, quick release pressure by adjusting the pressure valve to the vent.
12. After pressure gets released, open the pressure lid.
13. Slice and serve the pie warm and enjoy!

Per Serving: Calories 369, Carbs 26 g, Fats 25.5 g, Protein 16 g

Kale Sausage Breakfast

This is a delicious side dish recipe; it is a favorite of many who have tried it out. It cooks well in the Foodi.

Prep time 10 minutes/ Cook time 10 minutes/ Serves 4
Ingredients
- 1 medium sweet yellow onion
- 4 medium eggs
- 4 sausage links
- 2 cups kale, chopped
- 1 cup mushrooms
- Olive oil as required

Directions
1. Take Ninja Foodi Grill, arrange it over your kitchen platform, and open the top lid.
2. Arrange the grill grate and close the top lid.
3. Press "grill" and select the "high" grill function. Adjust the timer to 5 minutes and then press "start/stop." Ninja Foodi will start pre-heating.
4. Ninja Foodi is preheated and ready to cook when it starts to beep. After you hear a beep, open the top lid.
5. Arrange the sausages over the grill grate.
6. Close the top lid and cook for 2 minutes. Now open the top lid, flip the sausages.
7. Close the top lid and cook for three more minutes.
8. Take out the grilled sausages.
9. Take a multi-purpose pan and lightly grease it with some cooking oil. Spread the onion, mushrooms, and kale; add the grilled sausages and crack the eggs in between the sausages.
10. Open the lid and arrange the pan directly inside the pot.
11. Press "bake" and adjust the temperature to 350°F. Adjust the timer to 5 minutes and then press "start/stop."
12. Close the top lid and allow it to cook until the timer reads zero.
13. Serve warm.

Per Serving: Calories 236, Fats 12g, Carbs 17g, Protein 18g

Coconut Breakfast Bagels

This is very easy to make recipe, and it cooks in very little time. It takes less than 20 minutes to make; it takes 10 minutes of preparation time and 8 minutes of cooking.

Prep time 10 minutes/ Cook time 8 minutes/ Serves 4
Ingredients
- 1 cup fine sugar
- 2 tablespoons black coffee, prepared and cooled down
- 4 bagels, halved
- ¼ cup coconut milk

- 2 tablespoons coconut flakes

Directions
1. Take Ninja Foodi Grill, arrange it over your kitchen platform, and open the top lid.
2. Arrange the grill grate and close the top lid.
3. Press "grill" and select the "med" grill function. Adjust the timer to 4 minutes and then press "start/stop." Ninja Foodi will start pre-heating.
4. Ninja Foodi is preheated and ready to cook when it starts to beep. After you hear a beep, open the top lid.
5. Arrange 2 bagels over the grill grate.
6. Close the top lid and cook for 2 minutes. Now open the top lid, flip the bagels.
7. Close the top lid and cook for 2 more minutes.
8. Allow cooking until the timer reads zero. Divide into serving plates.
9. Grill the remaining bagels in a similar way. In a mixing bowl, whisk the remaining ingredients.
10. Serve the grilled bagels with the prepared sauce on top.

Per Serving: Calories 395, Fats 23g, Carbs 42.5g, Protein 18.5g

Pineapple French Toast

French toast has always been a thing for many since childhood. You can make them with variety by mix matching ingredients. Here, it is made with a pineapple and it is so delicious. You will love it.

Prep time 10 minutes/ Cook time 15 minutes/ Serves 5

Ingredients
- 10 bread slices
- ¼ cup sugar
- ¼ cup milk
- 3 large eggs
- 1 cup coconut milk
- 10 slices pineapple, peeled
- ½ cup coconut flakes
- Cooking spray

Directions
1. In a mixing bowl, whisk the coconut milk, sugar, eggs, and milk. Dip the bread in this mixture and set aside for about 2 minutes.
2. Take Ninja Foodi Grill, arrange it over your kitchen platform, and open the top lid.
3. Arrange the grill grate and close the top lid.
4. Press "grill" and select the "med" grill function. Adjust the timer to 4 minutes and then press "start/stop." Ninja Foodi will start pre-heating.
5. Ninja Foodi is preheated and ready to cook when it starts to beep. After you hear a beep, open the top lid.
6. Arrange half the bread slices over the grill grate.
7. Close the top lid and cook for 2 minutes. Now open the top lid, flip the slices.
8. Close the top lid and cook for 2 more minutes.
9. Allow cooking until the timer reads zero. Divide into serving plates.
10. Repeat with the remaining slices. And then grill the pineapple slices with the same amount of time (flipping after 2 minutes).
11. Serve warm with the grilled bread topped with some coconut flakes.

Per Serving: Calories 202, Fats 15g, Carbohydrates 49g, Protein 8g

Creamed French Toast

Prep time 10 minutes/ Cook time 4 minutes/ Serves 3
Ingredients
- Juice, ½ orange
- 3 slices challah bread
- 2 medium eggs
- ½ quart strawberries, quartered
- 1 tablespoon balsamic vinegar
- ¼ cup heavy cream
- 1 tablespoon honey
- 1 teaspoon orange zest
- ½ teaspoon vanilla extract
- ½ sprig rosemary
- Salt

Directions
1. Take a foil sheet and add the strawberries, balsamic vinegar, orange juice, rosemary, and zest. Fold edges to create a pocket.
2. In a mixing bowl, whisk the egg; add the cream, honey, vanilla, and a pinch of salt and whisk again.
3. Dip the bread slices to coat evenly in the mixture.
4. Take Ninja Foodi Grill, arrange it over your kitchen platform, and open the top lid.
5. Arrange the grill grate and close the top lid.
6. Press "grill" and select the "med" grill function. Adjust the timer to 4 minutes and then press "start/stop." Ninja Foodi will start pre-heating.
7. Ninja Foodi is preheated and ready to cook when it starts to beep. After you hear a beep, open the top lid.
8. Arrange the foil packet and bread slices over the grill grate.
9. Close the top lid and cook for 2 minutes. Now open the top lid, flip the flip.
10. Close the top lid and cook for 2 more minutes.
11. Allow cooking until the timer reads zero. Divide into serving plates.
12. Serve warm the bread with the strawberry mixture.

Per Serving: Calories 369, Fats 11.5g, Carbs 36g, Protein 15g

Cheesy Egg Bites

Having quick and easy breakfasts that can be made ahead of time can really be a game changer. You can make a batch of them on a Sunday night and reheat as needed throughout the week.

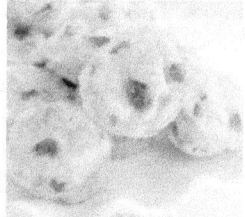

Prep time 5 minutes/ Cook time 20 minutes/ Serves 4
Ingredients
- 8 eggs
- ¼ cup heavy, whipping cream
- ½ cup shredded cheddar cheese

- Salt
- Freshly ground black pepper
- Cooking oil spray or extra-virgin olive oil, for greasing
- 1 cup water

Directions
1. In a large bowl, whisk the eggs until well beaten. Stir in the heavy cream and cheddar cheese. Season with salt and pepper.
2. Grease silicone baking molds or egg bite molds with the cooking oil spray and pour the egg mixture evenly into each one.
3. Pour the water into the pot. Place the reversible rack in the pot, making sure it is in steam position. Carefully lower the egg molds onto the rack. Assemble the pressure lid, making sure the pressure release valve is in the seal position.
4. Select pressure and set to high. Set time to 8 minutes. Select start/stop to begin.
5. When pressure cooking is complete, quick release the pressure by moving the pressure release valve to the vent position. Carefully remove the lid when the unit has finished releasing pressure. Drain any remaining water and top egg bites with more cheese (if using; if not, serve immediately or refrigerate until ready to serve).
6. Close the crisping lid. Select broil and set time to 3 minutes. Select start/stop to begin, checking after 2 minutes if the cheese is melted and slightly browned.
7. Remove the egg bites and serve immediately or refrigerate until ready to serve.

Per Serving: Calories 235, Fats 19g, Carbs 1g, Protein 15g

Everyday Poached Eggs

Eggs are such an easy way to add protein to a low-carb diet. Poached eggs are packed with flavor from that slightly runny yolk. They work with almost everything, and can be thrown onto salads, cauliflower rice bowls, and so much more. The possibilities are endless.

Prep time 3 minutes/ Cook time 4 minutes/ Serves 6

Ingredients
- 1 cup water
- Cooking oil spray
- 6 eggs
- Salt
- Freshly ground black pepper

Directions
1. Place the reversible rack in the pot, making sure it is in the steam position. Add the water to the pot.
2. Grease egg bite molds with the cooking oil spray. Carefully crack an egg into each mold. Place the egg bite mold onto the rack. Assemble the pressure lid, making sure the pressure release valve is in the seal position.
3. Select pressure and set to high. Set time to 4 minutes. Select start/stop to begin.
4. When pressure cooking is complete, naturally release the pressure for 2 minutes, then quick release any remaining pressure by moving the pressure release valve to the vent position. Carefully remove the lid when the unit has finished releasing pressure.
5. Season the eggs with salt and pepper and serve immediately.

Per Serving: Calories 72, Fats 5g, Carbs 1g, Protein 6g

Low-Carb Blueberry Muffins

A low-carb muffin and a cup of coffee can be taken in the morning or as an early afternoon snack. These keto-friendly blueberry muffins freeze well, so you can make a batch and save most of them for a rainy day.

Prep time 5 minutes/ Cook time 27 minutes/ Serves 6

Ingredients
- 2 cups water
- 1¼ cups almond flour
- ½ tablespoon baking powder
- Pinch salt
- ¼ cup coconut oil, melted
- 3 eggs
- 1 teaspoon vanilla extract
- 1 tablespoon stevia or low-carb sweetener of choice
- ½ cup fresh blueberries

Directions
1. Pour the water into the pot.
2. In a large bowl, combine the almond flour, baking powder, salt, coconut oil, eggs, vanilla, and stevia (if using). Gently fold in the blueberries.
3. Scoop batter evenly into 6 silicone muffin liners. Carefully arrange them on the rack. Lower rack into the pot in the steam position. Assemble the pressure lid, making sure the pressure release valve is in the seal position.
4. Select pressure and set to low. Set time to 10 minutes. Select start/stop to begin.
5. When pressure cooking is complete, naturally release the pressure for 5 minutes then quick release any remaining pressure by moving the pressure release valve to the vent position. Carefully remove the lid when the unit has finished releasing pressure. Remove the muffins from the pot and serve.

Per Serving: Calories 238, Fats 19g, Carbs 9g, Protein 7g

Veggie Frittata

Eggs and veggies make a great keto breakfast. This recipe is a great way to combine eggs and veggies and pull it all together in the form of a frittata, which makes not only a great breakfast but a wonderful light lunch or even an easy dinner. Mix up the veggies using whatever you have in your refrigerator, and be sure to experiment.

Prep time 10 minutes/ Cook time 1 hour 6 minutes/ Serves 6

Ingredients
- 2 tablespoons extra-virgin olive oil
- 1 onion, thinly sliced
- 1 garlic clove, minced
- ½ cup red bell pepper, chopped
- Cooking oil spray
- 12 eggs, beaten
- 1 cup chopped spinach
- 1 cup shredded cheddar cheese
- Salt

- Freshly ground black pepper
- 1 cup water

Directions

1. Select sear/sauté and add the olive oil to the pot. Once hot, add the onion and cook for 3 to 4 minutes. Add the garlic and continue to sauté, about 1 minute. Add the bell pepper and cook another 3 to 4 minutes. Transfer the vegetables to a bowl and let cool slightly.
2. Spray a round baking dish that fits into the pot with the cooking oil spray. Add the eggs and spinach and stir to combine. Add the cheddar cheese and stir to combine. Stir in the vegetables. Season with salt and pepper.
3. Wipe the pot clean. Place the reversible rack in the pot, making sure the rack is in the steam position. Cover the baking dish with aluminum foil and place it carefully on the rack. Pour the water into the pot. Assemble the pressure lid, making sure the pressure release valve is in the seal position.
4. Select pressure and set to high. Set time to 35 minutes. Select start/stop to begin.
5. When pressure cooking is complete, naturally release the pressure for 10 minutes then quick release any remaining pressure by moving the pressure release valve to the vent position. Carefully remove the lid when the unit has finished releasing pressure.
6. Serve the frittata or keep it warm until ready to serve.

Per Serving: Calories 260, Fats 20g, Carbs 4g, Protein 16g

Breakfast Casserole

This breakfast casserole is what you should think of when you think of brunch parties

Prep time 5 minutes/ Cook time 1 hour 8 minutes/ Serves 6

Ingredients

- 6 ounces ground breakfast sausage
- 12 eggs, beaten
- 1 can green chiles, diced
- 2 cups Monterey Jack cheese, shredded
- 1 cup heavy, whipping cream
- Salt
- Freshly ground black pepper
- Cooking oil spray
- 1 cup water

Directions

1. Select sear/sauté and add the breakfast sausage. Brown the sausage for 4 to 5 minutes, using a wooden spoon to break the meat into small pieces. Transfer the sausage to a bowl and let cool slightly. Wipe the pot clean.
2. In a large bowl, combine the eggs, chiles, cooked sausage, cheese, and cream. Season with salt and pepper.
3. Spray a round baking dish that fits into the pot with the cooking oil spray. Pour the egg mixture into the dish and cover with aluminum foil. Pour the water into the pot. Place the reversible rack in the pot, making sure rack is in the steam position. Assemble the pressure lid, making sure the pressure release valve is in the seal position.
4. Select pressure and set to high. Set time to 35 minutes. Select start/stop to begin.
5. When pressure cooking is complete, naturally release the pressure for 10 minutes then quick release any remaining pressure by moving the pressure release valve to the vent position. Carefully remove the lid when the unit has finished releasing pressure.
6. Remove the foil and top the casserole with more cheese.
7. Close the crisping lid. Select broil and set time to 6 minutes. Select start/stop to begin, checking after 5 minutes if the cheese is melted and slightly browned.

8. When cooking is complete, serve the casserole right away or keep warm until ready to serve.
Per Serving: Calories 468, Fats 40g, Carbs 4g, Protein 23g

Crustless Sausage and Mushroom Quiche

Sautéed mushrooms are good on everything, but they are especially good in the morning with some eggs and sausage. This crustless quiche is an easy casserole-like recipe that combines some flavors. It refrigerates well, so you can make it ahead of time and reheat before serving.

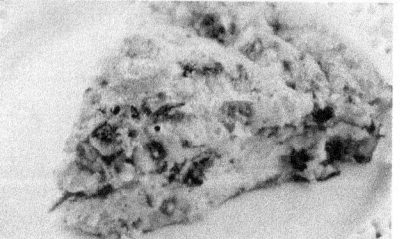

Prep time 5 minutes/ Cook time 54 minutes/ Serves 4
Ingredients
- 2 tablespoons unsalted butter
- 10 ounces sliced mushrooms
- 6 ounces ground breakfast sausage
- Salt
- Freshly ground black pepper
- 12 eggs
- ½ cup heavy, whipping cream
- 2 tablespoons chopped chives
- 1 cup shredded cheddar cheese
- Cooking oil spray

Directions
1. Select sear/sauté and add the butter. Once melted, add the mushrooms and stir well to combine. Cook 5 to 6 minutes, or until the mushrooms begin to brown. Add the sausage and cook another 5 to 6 minutes, stirring well to combine and cook the sausage through. Season with salt and pepper. Transfer to a bowl and let cool. Wipe the pot clean.
2. While the sausage and mushrooms cook, combine the eggs, cream, and chives in a large bowl. Season with salt and pepper.
3. Add the cooled mushrooms and sausage to the egg mixture and stir to combine. Add the cheese and stir well.
4. Spray a round baking dish with the cooking oil spray. Pour the egg mixture into the dish and cover with aluminum foil. Place the reversible rack in the pot, making sure the rack is in the steam position. Place the baking dish on the rack. Assemble the pressure lid, making sure the pressure release valve is in the seal position.
5. Select pressure and set to high. Set time to 25 minutes. Select start/stop to begin.
6. When pressure cooking is complete, naturally release the pressure for 5 minutes, then quick release any remaining pressure by moving the pressure release valve to the vent position. Carefully remove the lid when the unit has finished releasing pressure.
7. Remove the foil and serve immediately, or keep covered and refrigerate. Reheat before serving.
Per Serving: Calories 602, Fats 50g, Carbs 5g, Protein 33g

Mexican Breakfast Bowls

These Mexican Breakfast Bowls are great because most of the components can be made ahead of time, so when you're ready for breakfast all you have to do is reheat and assemble.

Prep time 10 minutes/ Cook time 14 minutes/ Serves 4
Ingredients
- 1 head cauliflower
- 2 tablespoons unsalted butter, divided
- Salt
- Freshly ground black pepper
- 8 eggs, beaten
- 1 cup shredded Barbacoa Beef
- ½ cup shredded Mexican-blend cheese
- ¼ cup sour cream
- 1 avocado, sliced
- 2 tablespoons fresh chopped cilantro

Directions
1. To rice the cauliflower, cut into smaller pieces and pulse in a food processor into a rice-like consistency. Alternatively, use a cheese grater to shred the cauliflower.
2. Select sear/sauté and add 1 tablespoon of butter. Once melted, add the cauliflower rice and season with salt and pepper. Sauté for 2 to 3 minutes.
3. Close the crisping lid. Select air crisp, set temperature to 390°F, and set time to 7 minutes. Select start/stop to begin, stirring the cauliflower rice halfway through cooking.
4. When cooking is complete, open the lid and push the cauliflower rice to the side. Select sear/sauté and add the remaining 1 tablespoon of butter to the pot. Once melted, pour in the eggs. Scramble the eggs, stirring occasionally, for 3 to 4 minutes, or until set to your liking. Season with salt and pepper.
5. Assemble the breakfast bowls by spooning cauliflower rice and eggs into bowls and topping with the beef. Sprinkle with the cheese and a dollop of sour cream. Layer avocado slices on top. Finish with a garnish of chopped cilantro.

Per Serving: Calories 461, Carbs 15g, Fat 33g, Protein 26g

Giant Pancake

This is a fun recipe that's a bit different from your everyday pancakes—it's one big pancake that is low in carbs and comes out like a fluffy cloud of breakfast goodness. This recipe is great because you just mix it together, pour it in the pot, and pressure cook it. Cut it into slices like a pie, and you're ready for breakfast.

Prep time 5 minutes/ Cook time 15 minutes/ Serves 6
Ingredients
- 1½ tablespoons unsalted butter, room temperature
- 1¼ cup almond flour
- 1 teaspoon baking powder
- 6 eggs, beaten
- ¾ cup heavy, whipping cream
- 1½ teaspoons vanilla extract

- 1 tablespoon Stevia or preferred low-carb sweetener
- Pinch salt
- Grease the pot well with the butter.

Directions
1. In a large bowl, combine the almond flour, baking powder, eggs, heavy cream, vanilla, low-carb sweetener, and salt.
2. Pour the pancake mixture into the pot. Assemble the pressure lid, making sure the pressure release valve is in the seal position.
3. Select pressure and set to low. Set time to 0 minutes. Select start/stop to begin.
4. After coming to pressure, the unit will show a water notification on the screen. Remove the pressure lid and lower the crisping lid. Select bake/roast and set temperature to 350 degrees for 5 minutes.
5. Let the pancake cool slightly before slicing and serving—simply flip the cooking pot over onto a cooling rack (the pancake should slide right out).

Per Serving: Calories 282, Fats 22g, Carbs 11g, Protein 10g

Morning Hashes

This is a straight forward and easy dish for anyone to try out, and with the Ninja Foodi, you are more likely to make it successfully, even if it is your first time.

Prep time 5 minutes/ Cook time 20 minutes/ Serves 2

Ingredients:
- 1 tablespoon unsalted butter
- ½ teaspoon dried thyme, crushed
- ½ cup cauliflower florets, boiled, chopped
- ½ small onion, chopped
- ½ cup of water
- Salt and black pepper
- ½ pound turkey meat, chopped
- ¼ cup heavy cream

Directions
1. Turn on the Ninja Foodi and press sauté.
2. Add butter and onions and sauté for 3 minutes.
3. Add cauliflowers and sauté for 2 minutes.
4. Add turkey, water, thyme and pepper.
5. Close the lid.
6. Set the Ninja Foodi to "Manual" at high pressure for 10 minutes, release the pressure quickly.
7. Open the lid and press broil.
8. Add heavy cream, cook for 2 minutes.
9. Serve and enjoy.

Per serving: Calories 151, Fats 11.6 g, Carbs 0.7 g, Protein 11.1 g

Scrambled Cheese Eggs with Broccoli

It is important that you start your day with an amazing meal that would fuel you for the rest of the day, and this meal is exactly that.

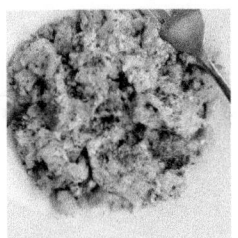

Prep time 10 minutes/ Cook time 8 minutes/ Serves 6

Ingredients:
- 2 tablespoons butter
- 12 ounces broccoli florets
- Salt and black pepper, to taste
- ¼ cup of water
- ¾ cup cheddar cheese, shredded
- 8 eggs
- 2 tablespoons milk

Directions
1. Turn on Ninja Foodi and select sauté.
2. Add butter, broccoli and sauté for 3 minutes.
3. Add water, pepper, and salt and close the lid.
4. Set the Ninja Foodi to "Manual" at high pressure for 7 minutes, release the pressure quickly.
5. Open the lid and select sauté.
6. Add eggs, milk and sauté for 2 minutes.
7. Add cheese and press "air crisp" at 320 degrees F.
8. Cook for 2 minutes and serve.

Per Serving: Calories 197, Fats 14.6 g, Carbs 4.7 g, Protein 12.7 g

Spinach Quiche

This Spinach Quiche is savory, and salty on the outside; they are very tender on the inside.

Prep time 15 minutes/ Cook time 33 minutes/ Serves 6

Ingredients:
- 1 tablespoon butter, melted
- 1 package frozen spinach, thawed
- 5 organic eggs, beaten
- Salt and black pepper
- 3 cups Monterey Jack cheese, shredded

Directions
1. Turn on Ninja Foodi and select sauté.
2. Add butter, spinach and sauté for 3 minutes.
3. Dish it out in a bowl.
4. Add eggs, cheese, salt, pepper to a bowl.
5. Transfer it into molds that were greased.
6. Place molds inside Ninja Foodi and press "bake/roast."
7. Set the timer to 30 minutes at 360 degrees F and press start.
8. Remove molds after the time and cut in equal-sized wedges.
9. Serve and enjoy.

Per Serving: Calories 349, Fats 27.8 g, Carbs 3.2 g, Protein 23 g

Mushroom Tofu

Tofu is an all-time vegetarian favorite for many. Cheers to a happy moment making this delicious mushroom tofu.

Prep time 15 minutes/ Cook time 15 minutes/ Serves 6
Ingredients:
- 8 tablespoons Parmesan cheese, shredded
- 2 cups fresh mushrooms, finely chopped
- 2 blocks tofu, pressed and cubed into 1-inch pieces
- Salt and black pepper, to taste
- 8 tablespoons butter

Directions
1. Take a bowl and add tofu, salt, pepper in it. Mix well.
2. Press sauté and add butter, tofu in a bowl and sauté for 5 minutes.
3. Add mushrooms, parmesan cheese and sauté for 3 minutes.
4. Press "air crisp" and cool for 7 minutes at 350 degrees F.
5. Serve and enjoy.

Per Serving: Calories 211, Fats 18.5 g, Carbs 2 g, Protein 11.5 g

Bacon and Veggies

Just 25 minutes and you should have something and tasty to munch on anytime. The bacon and veggies recipe is not fattening so you have as much as you want.

Prep time 10 minutes/ Cook time 25 minutes/ Serves 4
Ingredients:
- 1 green bell pepper, seeded, chopped
- 4 bacon slices
- ½ cup Parmesan Cheese
- 1 tablespoon avocado mayonnaise
- 2 scallions, chopped

Directions
1. Place bacon at the bottom of Ninja Foodi.
2. Top it with avocado mayonnaise, scallions, bell peppers, and Parmesan cheese.
3. Press "bake/roast" and set the timer to 25 minutes at 365 degrees F.
4. Dish out and serve.

Per Serving: Calories 197, Fats 13.8 g, Carbs 4.7 g, Protein 14.3 g

Scrambled Onion Tofu

The Scrambled Onion Tofu is an amazing recipe filled with lots of flavor that will make you enjoy it.

Prep time 10 minutes/ Cook time 12 minutes/ Serves 4
Ingredients:
- 4 tablespoons butter
- 2 blocks tofu, pressed and cubed into 1-inch pieces
- Salt and black pepper to taste
- 1 cup cheddar cheese, grated
- 2 medium onions, sliced

Directions
1. Take a bowl and add tofu, salt, pepper in it. Mix well.
2. Turn on the Ninja Foodi and select sauté.
3. Add onions, butter and sauté for 3 minutes.
4. Add tofu and cook for 2 minutes.
5. Add cheddar cheese and lock the lid.
6. Set Ninja Foodi on "air crisp" to 3 minutes at 340 degrees F.
7. Serve and enjoy.

Per Serving: Calories 184, Fats 12.7 g, Carbs 6.3 g, Protein 12.2 g

Omelet with Pepperoni

The thing a lot of people are usually curious about is if the ceramic pot of the Foodi would be as effective as the stainless-steel pot of the Instant Pot in making this recipe. I can assure you, as it is proven, that the Foodi does as well as the Instant Pot.

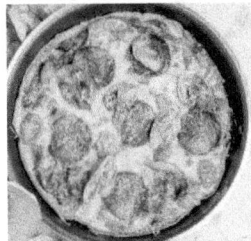

Prep time 10 minutes/ Cook time 30 minutes/ Serves 4
Ingredients:
- 4 tablespoons heavy cream
- 15 pepperoni slices
- 2 tablespoons butter
- Salt and black pepper, to taste
- 6 eggs

Directions
1. Take a bowl and add eggs, heavy cream, salt, pepper, pepperoni and mix well.
2. Turn on the Ninja Foodi and select sauté.
3. Add butter, egg mixture and sauté for 3 minutes.
4. Flip the side and lock the lid.
5. Set it on "air crisp" and cook for 2 minutes at 350 degrees F.
6. Serve and enjoy.

Per Serving: Calories 141, Fats 11.3 g, Carbs 0.6 g, Protein 8.9 g

Bok Choy Samba with Bacon

This Bok Choy Samba with Bacon satisfies in tastes, nutrients, and flavor and is even healthier than the usual Bok Choy.

Prep time 10 minutes/ Cook time 14 minutes/ Serves 6

Ingredients:
- 4 bacon slices
- 2 tablespoons olive oil
- 8 tablespoons cream
- 8 bok choy, sliced
- 1 cup Parmesan cheese, grated
- Salt and black pepper, to taste

Directions
1. Season the bok choy with salt and pepper.
2. Turn on Ninja Foodi and select sauté.
3. Add olive oil, bacon slices and sauté for 5 minutes.
4. Add cream, seasoned bok choy and sauté for 6 minutes.
5. Top with Parmesan cheese and lock the lid.
6. Set it on "air crisp" for 3 minutes at 350 degrees F.
7. Dish out and enjoy.

Per Serving: Calories 112, Fats 4.9 g, Carbs 1.9 g, Protein 3 g

CHAPTER 3: POULTRY RECIPES

Chicken

Hot Chicken Wings

It is also rich in fresh flavors that make eaters want more of it! Many people love wings as a favorite as they are juicy and affordable! Get it today!

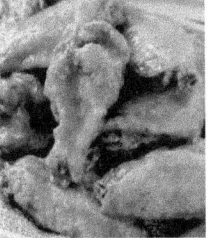

Prep time 10 minutes/ Cook time 15 minutes/ Serves 4
Ingredients
- 8 chicken wings
- 1 tbsp ranch salad mix
- 1 tbsp garlic powder
- 1 tbsp onion powder
- 1 tbsp cayenne pepper
- ½ tsp paprika
- Cooking spray

Directions:
1. Preheat your Ninja Air fryer to 380 degrees F.
2. Combine the paprika, ranch salad mix, onion powder, garlic powder, and cayenne pepper in a bowl.
3. Pour the seasoning all over the chicken and oil with cooking spray.
4. Place in the air fryer basket and cook for 15 minutes.
5. After half of the cooking time, shake the wings. Oil the chicken again with cooking spray and continue cooking until the wings are crispy. Serve hot.

Per serving: Calories 105, Carbs 4g, Fats 3g, Protein 18g

Basil & Cheddar Stuffed Chicken

This recipe is among the fastest and easiest and this is the reason why you will love it! It is amazing and it tastes good! No matter the diet that you could be on, this meal tastes good. It can be made for anyone that is not on any diet and they will not be disappointed.

Prep time 6 minutes/ Cook time 12 minutes/ Serves 4
Ingredients:
- 2 large chicken breasts, skinless
- 4 slices cheddar cheese
- A handful of fresh basil leaves
- 4 cherry tomatoes, halved
- Salt and pepper to taste
- 2 tbsp olive oil

Directions:
1. Preheat your Ninja Air fryer to 370 degrees F.

2. With a sharp knife, cut a slit into the side of each chicken breast.
3. Put 2 slices of cheese, 3-4 basil leaves, and 4 cherry tomato halves into each slit.
4. Use toothpicks to keep the chicken breasts closed.
5. Season the meat with salt and pepper, and brush with some olive oil.
6. Grease the air fryer basket with the remaining olive oil and place the chicken breasts in the basket; cook for 12 minutes. After 6 minutes, turn the breasts over.
7. Once ready, leave to sit the chicken breasts, then slice each one in half and serve with salad.

Per serving: Calories 354, Carbs 6g, Fats 18g, Protein 34g

Honey-Glazed Chicken Kabobs

This is a common recipe that is loved by many because its taste is amazing! You need to make this delicious recipe and you will love it all the way! The recipe itself is very easy to prepare!

Prep time 5 minutes/ Cook time 15 minutes/ Serves 4
Ingredients:
- 4 chicken breasts, skinless, cubed
- 4 tbsp honey
- Juice from 1 Lime
- ½ tsp ground paprika
- Salt and pepper to taste

Directions:
1. Preheat your Ninja Air Fryer to 360 degrees F.
2. In a large bowl, combine the honey, soy sauce, lime juice, paprika, salt, and pepper.
3. Add in the chicken cubes and toss to coat.
4. Load 8 small skewers with honey-glazed chicken. Lay the kabobs into the air fryer basket and cook for 15 minutes. After 8 minutes, turn the kabobs over.
5. Drizzle the remaining honey sauce and serve with sautéed veggies.

Per serving: Calories 356, Carbs 53.6g, Fats 7g, Protein 20g

Chicken with Prunes

This chicken will leave you wanting for more when you eat it because it is so delicious! This is not the right thing for you if you are the kind of people that dislike food touching each other on the plate or if you usually eat item by item on your meal! However, this should not discourage you. You will enjoy the meal!

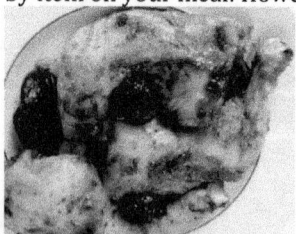

Prep time 10 minutes/ Cook time 55 minutes/ Serves 6
Ingredients:
- 1 whole chicken, 3 lb.
- ½ cup pitted prunes
- 3 minced cloves of garlic
- 2 tbsp capers
- 2 bay leaves

- 2 tbsp red wine vinegar
- 2 tbsp olive oil
- 1 tbsp dried oregano
- ¼ cup packed brown sugar
- 1 tbsp chopped fresh parsley
- Salt and black pepper to taste

Directions:
1. In a big and deep bowl, mix the prunes, olives, capers, garlic, olive oil, bay leaves, oregano, vinegar, salt, and pepper.
2. Spread the mixture on the bottom of a baking tray, and place the chicken.
3. Preheat the Ninja Air fryer to 360° F. Sprinkle a little bit of brown sugar on top of the chicken and cook for 45 - 55 minutes on Air Fry mode. Garnish with fresh parsley.

Per serving: Calories 288, Carbs 44g, Fats 18g, Protein 39g

Chicken Burgers with Avocado

This recipe is healthy and the simplest that you will make ever! It takes just 15 minutes to get it ready and more so it is nutrients-packed!

Prep time 5 minutes/ Cook time 10 minutes/ Serves 8

Ingredients:
- 1 lb. ground chicken
- 1 red onion, chopped
- 1 egg, beaten
- 4 buns, halved
- 1 small red potato, shredded
- A pinch of ground cumin
- A pinch of ground chili
- Fresh cilantro, chopped
- Salt and pepper to taste
- 1 Avocado, sliced
- ½ cup mayonnaise
- 1 tomato, sliced
- Cooking spray

Directions:
1. Preheat your Ninja Air fryer to 360 degrees F.
2. Mix the chicken, onion, egg, potato, cumin, chili, cilantro, salt, and pepper in a large bowl with your hands until you have an even burger mixture.
3. Shape the mixture into 8 patties.
4. Grease your air fryer basket with cooking spray.
5. Arrange the burgers onto the basket. Cook for 10 minutes. After 5 minutes, shake the patties.
6. To assemble your burgers, spread mayonnaise on the bottom of each half of the buns, top with a chicken patty, then put over a tomato slice.
7. Cover with the other half of the buns and arrange on a serving platter to serve.

Per serving: Calories 414, Carbs 27g, Fats 27g, Protein 16g

Crunchy Chicken Schnitzels

This recipe is one of the recipes that you are likely not to share with anyone! It is simply amazing!

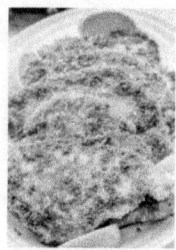

Prep time 5 minutes/ Cook time 10 minutes/ Serves 4
Ingredients:
- 4 chicken breasts, boneless
- 1 cup flour
- 2 eggs, beaten
- 1 cup breadcrumbs
- Salt and pepper to taste
- 2 tbsp fresh parsley, chopped
- 4 slices cold butter
- 4 slices lemon
- Cooking spray

Directions:
1. Preheat your Ninja Air fryer to 380 degrees F.
2. Combine the breadcrumbs with the parsley in a dish and set aside.
3. Season the chicken with salt and pepper.
4. Coat in flour; shake off any excess.
5. Dip the coated chicken into the beaten egg followed by breadcrumbs.
6. Spray the schnitzels with cooking spray.
7. Put them into the air fryer basket and cook for 10 minutes.
8. After 5 minutes, turn the schnitzels over.
9. Arrange the schnitzels on a serving platter and place the butter and lemon slices over to serve.

Per serving: Calories 513, Carbs 44g, Fats 28g, Protein 49g

Cordon Bleu Chicken

You can bet that this recipe is awesome! The chicken is full of nutrients and you will enjoy every bit of it.

Prep time 10 minutes/ Cook time 25 minutes/ Serves 4
Ingredients:
- 4 skinless and boneless chicken breasts
- 4 slices ham
- 4 slices Swiss cheese
- 3 tbsp all-purpose flour
- 4 tbsp butter
- 1 tsp paprika
- 1 tsp chicken bouillon granules
- ½ cup dry white wine
- 1 cup heavy whipping cream

Directions:
1. Preheat the Ninja Air fryer to 380° F.

2. Pound the chicken breasts and put a slice of ham and then a slice of swiss cheese on each of the breasts. Fold the edges over the filling and secure the sides with toothpicks.
3. In a medium bowl, combine the paprika and the flour and coat the chicken pieces.
4. Fry the chicken for 20 minutes on Air Fry mode.
5. Meanwhile, in a large skillet over medium heat, melt the butter and add the bouillon and the wine. Reduce the heat to low.
6. Add in the heavy cream and let simmer for 20-25 minutes. When the chicken is done, remove to a serving platter and drizzle with the sauce. Serve hot.
Per serving: Calories 317, Carbs 48g, Fats 22g, Protein 35g

Rosemary Lemon Chicken

You can bet that this recipe is awesome! The chicken is full of nutrients and you will enjoy every bit of it.

Prep time 5 minutes/ Cook time 6 minutes/ Serves 2
Ingredients:
- 2 chicken breasts
- 1 tsp minced ginger
- 2 rosemary sprigs
- ½ lemon, cut into wedges
- 1 tbsp soy sauce
- ½ tbsp olive oil
- 1 tbsp oyster sauce
- 3 tbsp brown sugar

Directions:
1. Place the ginger, soy sauce, and olive oil, in a bowl. Add the chicken and coat well.
2. Cover the bowl and refrigerate for 30 minutes.
3. Preheat the air fryer to 370 F. Transfer the marinated chicken to the air fryer basket.
4. Cook for about 6 minutes on Air Fry mode.
5. Mix the oyster sauce, rosemary and brown sugar in a small bowl. Pour the sauce over the chicken. Arrange the lemon wedges in the dish. Return to the air fryer and cook for 13 more minutes on Air Fry mode.
Per serving: Calories 275, Carbs 19g, Fats 7.6g, Protein 36g

Greek-Style Chicken

Rosemary Lemon Chicken is amazing and it tastes good with any diet! No matter the diet that you could be on, this meal tastes good.

Prep time 10 minutes/ Cook time 45 minutes/ Serves 6
Ingredients:
- 1 whole chicken, cut in pieces
- 3 garlic cloves, minced
- ½ cup olive oil

- ½ cup white wine
- 1 tbsp fresh rosemary
- 1 tbsp chopped fresh oregano
- 1 tbsp fresh thyme
- Juice from 1 lemon
- Salt and black pepper

Directions:
1. Preheat the Ninja Air fryer to 380° F.
2. In a large bowl, combine the garlic, rosemary, thyme, olive oil, lemon juice, oregano, salt, and pepper.
3. Mix all ingredients very well and spread the mixture into the air fryer basket.
4. Stir in the chicken. Sprinkle with wine and cook for 45 minutes on Air Fry mode.

Per serving: Calories 283, Carbs 34g, Fats 12g, Protein 27g

Asian-Style Chicken

You need to make this delicious recipe and you will love it all the way! The recipe itself is very easy to prepare!

Prep time 10 minutes/ Cook time 25 minutes/ Serves 4

Ingredients:
- 1 lb. chicken, cut in stripes
- 2 tomatoes, cubed
- 3 green peppers, cut in stripes
- 1 tbsp cumin powder
- 1 large onion
- 2 tbsp oil
- 1 tbsp mustard
- 1 pinch ginger
- 1 pinch fresh and chopped coriander
- Salt and black pepper

Directions:
1. Heat the oil in a deep pan. Add in the mustard, onion, ginger, cumin and green chili peppers. Sauté the mixture for 2-3 minutes.
2. Then, add the tomatoes, coriander, and salt and keep stirring.
3. Preheat the Ninja Air fryer to 380° F.
4. Coat the chicken with oil, salt, and pepper and cook for 25 minutes on Air Fry mode.
5. Remove from the Air Fryer and pour the sauce over and around.

Per serving: Calories 313, Carbs 64g, Fats 14g, Protein 31g

Crumbed Sage Chicken Scallopini

Apart from the delicious taste, this recipe is quick and easy to make! This is one recipe that you can prepare many times and not be bored because apart from being delicious, it also simple to prepare. Who doesn't love a recipe that is easy to make? NOBODY!

Prep time 3 minutes/ Cook time 7 minutes/ Serves 4
Ingredients:
- 4 chicken breasts, skinless and boneless
- 3 oz breadcrumbs
- 2 tbsp grated Parmesan cheese
- 2 oz flour
- 2 eggs, beaten
- 1 tbsp fresh, chopped sage
- Cooking spray

Directions:
1. Preheat the Ninja Air fryer to 370 degrees F.
2. Place some plastic wrap underneath and on top of the chicken breasts.
3. Using a rolling pin beat the meat until it becomes fragile.
4. In a small bowl, combine the Parmesan, sage, and breadcrumbs.
5. Dip the chicken in the egg first, and then in the sage mixture.
6. Spray with cooking oil and arrange the meat in the air fryer.
7. Cook for 7 minutes on Air Fry mode.

Per serving: Calories 218, Carbs 8.9g, Fats 5.9g, Protein 30.4g

Chicken Tenders with Broccoli & Rice

Do you love Broccoli? Do you love chicken? If you answered yes to both questions then this is the perfect meal for you because it brings in the two different flavors and the result is amazing!

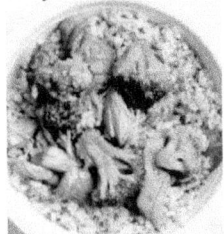

Prep time 10 minutes/ Cook time 1 hour/ Serves 3
Ingredients:
- 1-pound chicken tenderloins
- 1 package instant long grain rice
- 1 cup chopped broccoli
- 2 cups water
- 1 can condensed cream chicken soup
- 1 tbsp minced garlic

Directions:
1. Preheat the Air Fryer to 390° F, and place the chicken quarters in the Air Fryer.
2. Season with salt, pepper and a tbsp of oil and cook for 30 minutes on Roast mode.
3. Meanwhile, in a large bowl, mix rice, water, minced garlic, soup, and broccoli.
4. Combine the mixture very well.
5. Remove the chicken from the Air fryer and place it on a platter to drain.
6. Spread the rice mixture on the bottom of the dish and place the chicken on top of the rice. Cook again for 30 minutes on Roast mode.

Per serving: Calories 256, Carbs 29g, Fats 15g, Protein 23g

Buttermilk Chicken Thighs

This recipe is rich in fresh flavors that will make you want more! The mouthwatering sauce used to coat the chicken thighs is made up of cayenne pepper, black pepper, salt, and buttermilk.

Prep time 5 minutes/ Cook time 18 minutes/ Serves 6

Ingredients:
- 1 ½ lb. chicken thighs
- 1 tsp cayenne pepper
- 3 tsp salt divided
- 2 cups flour
- 2 tsp black pepper
- 1 tbsp paprika
- 1 tbsp baking powder
- 2 cups buttermilk

Directions:
1. Rinse and pat dry the chicken thighs. Place the chicken thighs in a bowl.
2. Add cayenne pepper, 2 tsp salt, black pepper, and buttermilk, and stir to coat well.
3. Refrigerate for 4 hours. Preheat the Ninja Air fryer to 350 degrees F.
4. In another bowl, mix the flour, paprika, 1 tsp salt, and baking powder.
5. Dredge half of the chicken thighs, one at a time, in the flour, and then place on a lined dish. Cook for 18 minutes on Air Fry mode, flipping once halfway through.
6. Repeat with the other batch.

Per serving: Calories 322, Carbs 36.3g, Fats 4.2g, Protein 32.7g

Roasted Crisp Whole Chicken

Roasted chicken is a favorite to many because it is so sweet and this recipe is no exception! The lemon gives the recipe another good taste which improves the recipe!

Prep time 10 minutes/ Cook time 25 minutes/ Serves 2

Ingredients:
- 1 whole Cornish Hen
- ½ tsp seasoned salt
- Juice of ½ lemon
- 1 tbsp honey
- ¼ cup hot water
- ¼ teaspoon salt
- ½ teaspoon whole peppercorns
- 1 sprigs of fresh thyme
- 2 cloves of garlic
- 1 tsp canola oil

Directions

1. Combine lemon juice, honey, water, salt, peppercorns, thyme, and garlic in pot.
2. Season the chicken inside, outside and underneath the skin with seasoned salt.
3. Place the chicken in the air crisp basket then place into the pot.
4. Install pressure lid. Close pot, choose high, and cook for 15 minutes.
5. Once done cooking, do a quick release. Remove pressure lid.
6. Brush the chicken with canola oil
7. Close the crisping lid and select roast.
8. Set the time for 15 minutes and halfway through cooking time turn chicken over.
9. The juices in the bottom of the cooking pot make a delicious sauce.

Per Serving: Calories 196, Fats 6.3g, Carbs 10.5g, protein 24.2g

Ginger-Balsamic Glazed Chicken

This is a common recipe that is loved by many because its taste is amazing! You need to make this delicious recipe and you will love it all the way!

Prep time 10 minutes/ Cook time 15 minutes/ Serves 2

Ingredients:
- 4 chicken thighs, skinless
- ¼ cup balsamic vinegar
- 1 ½ tablespoons mustard
- 1 tablespoon ginger garlic paste
- 4 cloves of garlic, minced
- 1-inche fresh ginger root
- 2 tablespoons honey
- Salt and pepper to taste

Directions
1. Place all ingredients in the Ninja Foodi. Stir to combine everything.
2. Install pressure lid. Close Ninja Foodi, press the manual button, choose high settings, and set time to 15 minutes.
3. Once done cooking, do a quick release. Remove pressure lid.
4. Mix and turnover chicken.
5. Cover, press roast, and roast for 5 minutes.
6. Serve and enjoy.

Per Serving: Calories 476; Carbs12.5g, Protein 32.4g, Fats 32.9g

Tasty Sesame-Honeyed Chicken

Love chicken? If yes then this is one of the chicken recipes that you should not miss. It is so sweet and yummy!

Prep time 4 minutes/ Cook time 16 minutes/ Serves 2

Ingredients:
- 1 tablespoon olive oil
- ½ onion, diced

- 2 cloves of garlic, minced
- 1-pound chicken breasts
- ¼ cup soy sauce
- 2 tbsp ketchup
- 1 tsp sesame oil
- ¼ cup honey
- ½ teaspoon red pepper flakes
- 1 tablespoon cornstarch + 1 ½ tablespoons water
- Green onions for garnish
- 1 tablespoon sesame seeds for garnish

Directions
1. Press the sauté button on the Ninja Foodi and heat the oil. Stir in the onion and garlic until fragrant.
2. Add the chicken breasts. Allow to sear on all sides for three minutes.
3. Stir in the soy sauce, ketchup, sesame oil, honey, and red pepper flakes.
4. Install pressure lid. Close Ninja Foodi, press the pressure button, choose high settings, and set time to 10 minutes.
5. Once done cooking, do a quick release.
6. Open the lid and press the sauté button. Stir in the cornstarch slurry and allow to simmer until the sauce thickens.
7. Garnish with green onions and sesame seeds last.
8. Serve and enjoy.

Per Serving: Calories 568, Carbs 49.1g, protein 50.9g, fats 34.6g

Traditional Chicken 'n Dumplings

The chicken 'n Dumplings, apart from being delicious it is also soft and eaten with ease. The tomatoes bring in the sweet flavor!

Prep time 5 minutes/ Cook time 25 minutes/ Serves 2

Ingredients:
- 1-pound chicken breasts, cut into cubes
- 2 cloves of garlic, minced
- ½ cup chopped onion
- ½ cup chopped celery
- ½ teaspoon dried thyme
- ½ tablespoon bouillon
- 1 cup frozen vegetables, peas and carrots
- 1 ½ cups chicken stock
- 1 can cream, chicken
- Salt and pepper to taste
- ½ can southern homestyle biscuits
- 2 tbsp parsley, chopped

Directions
1. Press the sauté button on the Ninja Foodi and stir in the chicken, garlic, onion, celery, and thyme. Stir constantly and allow the onions to sweat.
2. Stir in bouillon, vegetables, stock, and cream of chicken. Stir in the cream of chicken and season with salt and pepper to taste. Allow to simmer for a few minutes. Add the biscuits on top.
3. Install pressure lid. Close Ninja Foodi, press the pressure button, choose high settings, and set time to 15 minutes.

4. Once done cooking, do a quick release.
5. Remove pressure lid. Cover, press roast, and roast for 5 minutes at 400oF.
6. Garnish with parsley.
7. Serve and enjoy.

Per Serving: Calories 726; carbs 51.2g, protein 63.8g, fats 29.6g

Garlic Chicken in Creamy Tuscan Style

This is recipe is made full of flavor and made from ingredients that are addictive-free. It also contains all the nutrients that are needed for various body functions. Try it today!

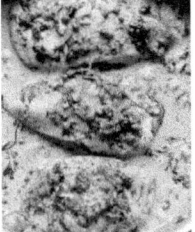

Prep time 5 minutes/ Cook time 15 minutes/ Serves 2

Ingredients:
- 1 tablespoon olive oil
- 1-pound skinless chicken breasts, halved, pounded
- 2 cloves, garlic, minced
- ½ tablespoon Italian seasoning
- ½ teaspoon salt
- 1/3 cup chicken stock
- 1/3 cup heavy cream
- 1/3 cup parmesan cheese
- ¼ cup sun-dried tomato

Directions
1. Press the sauté button on the Ninja Foodi and sear the chicken breasts on all sides.
2. Stir in the garlic, Italian seasoning, and salt.
3. Pour in the chicken stock and the rest of the ingredients.
4. Install pressure lid. Close Ninja Foodi, press the pressure button, choose high settings, and set time to 10 minutes.
5. Once done cooking, do a quick release.
6. Serve and enjoy.

Per Serving: Calories 521; carbs 10.8g, protein 59.9g, fats 26.5g

Green Curry Chicken Thai Style

It has several but very amazing ingredients which make it deliciously spicy. The recipes include coconut milk, cumin powder, onion, Thai green curry paste and many others. It is finger licking good!

Prep time 4 minutes/ Cook time 15 minutes/ Serves 2

Ingredients:
- 1 tablespoon Thai green curry paste
- 1/3 cup coconut milk
- ½ teaspoon coriander powder
- ½ teaspoon cumin powder

- 1/3-pound chicken breasts, bones removed and cut into chunks
- ¼ cup chicken broth
- 1 tablespoon fish sauce
- ¼ tablespoon sear button sugar
- ½ tablespoon lime juice
- 1 lime leaves, crushed
- ¼ cup bamboo shoots, sliced
- ¼ cup onion, cubed
- Salt and pepper to taste
- 1/3 cup green bell pepper
- 1/3 cup zucchini, sliced
- 2 tbsp Thai basil leaves

Directions
1. Press the sauté button on the Ninja Foodi. Place the Thai green curry paste and the coconut milk. Stir until the mixture bubbles. Stir in the coriander and cumin powder and cook for 30 seconds.
2. Stir in the chicken and coconut broth. Season with fish sauce, sear button sugar, lime juice, bamboo shoots, lime leaves, and onion. Season with salt and pepper to taste.
3. Install pressure lid. Close Ninja Foodi, press the manual button, choose high settings, and set time to 10 minutes.
4. Once done cooking, do a quick release. Open the lid and press the sauté button. Stir in the green bell pepper, zucchini, and basil leaves. Allow to simmer for at least 5 minutes to cook the vegetables.
5. Serve and enjoy.

Per Serving: Calories 208, carbs 9 g, protein 16 g, fats 12g

Savory 'n Aromatic Chicken Adobo

Do you love chicken? If yes to then this is the perfect meal for you because it brings in different flavors and the result is amazing! This recipe is spiced a little so as to give it more sweet taste!

Prep time 5 minutes/ Cook time 20 minutes/ Serves 2

Ingredients:
- 1-pound boneless chicken thighs
- ¼ cup white vinegar
- ½ cup water
- ¼ cup soy sauce
- ½ head garlic, peeled and smashed
- 2 bay leaves
- ½ teaspoon pepper
- 1 tsp oil

Directions
1. Place all ingredients in the Ninja Foodi.
2. Install pressure lid. Close Ninja Foodi, press the pressure button, choose high settings, and set time to 10 minutes.
3. Once done cooking, do a quick release.
4. Open the lid and press the sauté button. Allow the sauce to reduce so that the chicken is fried slightly in its oil, around 10 minutes.
5. Serve and enjoy.

Per Serving: Calories 713, carbs 3.2g, protein 43.9g, fats 58.3g

Duck

Duck with Asparagus

This recipe is definitely so delicious just like many poultry recipes. It is so nutritious with protein, B vitamins, iron, zinc and iron from the duck legs.

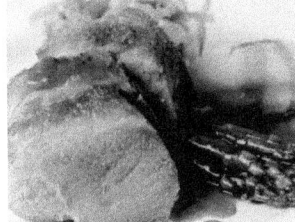

Prep time 5 minutes/ Cook time 25 minutes/ Serves 4
Ingredients:
- 2 duck legs, boneless
- 2 shallots, chopped
- 2 tablespoons butter
- 1 tablespoon sweet paprika
- 1 tablespoon tomato paste
- ½ cup chicken stock
- 1 bunch asparagus, trimmed, halved
- 1 tablespoon dill, chopped

Directions:
1. Set the Foodi on Sauté mode, add the butter, melt it, add the shallots and the duck and brown for 5 minutes.
2. add the rest of the ingredients, put the pressure lid on and cook on High for 20 minutes.
3. Release the pressure fast for 5 minutes, divide everything between plates and serve.

Per Serving: calories 254, fat 4.6g, carbs 18.4g, protein 30g

Parsley Duck and Fennel

This Parsley Duck and Fennel recipe is perfectly cooked to bring out the sweet flavors and healthy nutrients in its ingredients. It can be served alongside favorite side dish.

Prep time 10 minutes/ Cook time 25 minutes/ Serves 4
Ingredients:
- 2 duck breasts, boneless, skinless, halved
- 1 tablespoon olive oil
- 1 yellow onion, chopped
- 1 cup tomato sauce
- 2 fennel bulbs, shredded
- 2 teaspoons soy sauce
- Salt and black pepper to the taste

Directions:
1. Set the Foodi on Sauté mode, add the oil, heat it up, add the onion and sauté for 5 minutes.
2. Add the meat and the other ingredients, put the pressure lid on and cook on High for 20 minutes.
3. Release the pressure naturally for 10 minutes, divide everything between plates and serve.

Per Serving: calories 274, fat 14.4g, carbs 16.4g, protein 10.4g

Duck with Berries Mix

The Duck with Berries Mix is made using simple ingredients. It has all one can wish for in a nice meal. It is big in size and not like the small sizes served in restaurants. You will enjoy every bit of this amazing recipe!

Prep time 10 minutes/ Cook time 25 minutes/ Serves 4
Ingredients:
- 1-pound duck breast, skinless, boneless, halved
- 2 tablespoons butter, melted
- 1 cup blackberries
- 1 teaspoon sweet paprika
- Salt and black pepper
- 1 cup chicken stock
- 2 spring onions, chopped
- 2 tablespoons cilantro, chopped

Directions:
1. Set the Foodi on Sauté mode, add the butter, heat it up, add the onion the meat and brown for 5 minutes.
2. Add the berries and the remaining ingredients, put the pressure lid on and cook on High for 20 minutes.
3. Release the pressure naturally for 10 minutes, divide the mix between plates and serve.

Per Serving: calories 319, fat 17.4g, carbs 11.4g, protein 15.9g

Garlic Duck and Apples

Garlic Duck and Apples is a simple meal that has lots of flavor. Can't forget to mention that it very nutritious!

Prep time 10 minutes/ Cook time 30 minutes/ Serves 4
Ingredients:
- 2 duck legs, boneless
- 1 tablespoon avocado oil
- 2 garlic cloves, minced
- 1 tablespoon cilantro, chopped
- 2 apples, cored and cut into wedges
- ¾ cup white wine
- 1 teaspoon chili powder
- Salt and black pepper to the taste

Directions:
1. Put the reversible rack in the Foodi, add the baking pan and grease it with the oil.
2. Add the duck, the garlic and the other ingredients, set the machine on Baking mode and cook at 380 degrees F for 30 minutes.
3. Divide everything between plates and serve.

Per Serving: calories 170, fat 3g, carbs 17.7g, protein 11.5g

Thyme Duck

This is one of the easiest recipes to make. It has only six ingredients and only takes only 30 minutes to be ready! It tastes so good and is a good treat for you and your guests.

Prep time 10 minutes/ Cook time 30 minutes/ Serves 4
Ingredients:
- 2 duck legs, boneless, cubed
- 2 tablespoons butter, melted
- Salt and black pepper
- 1 teaspoon thyme, dried
- 1 cup tomatoes, halved
- 1 tablespoon parsley, chopped

Directions:
1. Set the Foodi on Sauté mode, add the oil, heat it up, add the meat and thyme and brown for 5 minutes.
2. Add the rest of the ingredients except the parsley, put the pressure lid on and cook on High for 25 minutes.
3. Release the pressure naturally for 10 minutes, divide the mix between plates, sprinkle the parsley on top and serve.

Per Serving: calories 127, fat 8.1g, carbs 2g, protein 11.4g

Turkey

Hot Turkey Cutlets

It's a traditional bird that is usually enjoyed during holidays, especially Thanksgiving. There is much more to it than just its great taste. It has lots of proteins, way more than chicken and beef!

Prep time 10 minutes/ Cook time 15 minutes/ Serves 4
Ingredients
- 1 teaspoon Greek seasoning
- 1-pound turkey cutlets
- 2 tablespoons olive oil
- 1 teaspoon turmeric powder
- ½ cup almond flour

Directions
1. Take a bowl and add Greek seasoning, turmeric powder, almond flour and mix well
2. Dredge turkey cutlets in the bowl and let it sit for 30 minutes
3. Set your Ninja Foodi to Sauté mode and add oil, let it heat up
4. Add cutlets and Sauté for 2 minutes
5. Lock lid and cook on Low-Medium Pressure for 20 minutes
6. Release pressure naturally over 10 minutes
7. Take the dish out, serve and enjoy!

Per Serving: Calories: 340, Fats 19g, Carbs 3.7g, Protein 36g

Turkey Potato Pie

This healthy and tasteful recipe is one of the easy go-to recipes. You will enjoy every bit of it!

Prep time 10 minutes/ Cook time 26 minutes/ Serves 6

Ingredients:
- 1 onion, diced
- 2 garlic cloves, minced
- 2 pounds boneless turkey breasts, cut into 1-inch cubes
- 2 Yukon Gold potatoes, diced
- 1 cup chicken broth
- ½ stick unsalted butter
- ½ teaspoon sea salt
- ½ teaspoon black pepper
- 2 cups mixed vegetables of your choice
- ½ cup heavy, whipping cream
- 1 refrigerated piecrust

Directions:
1. Take Ninja Foodi multi-cooker, arrange it over a cooking platform, and open the top lid.
2. In the pot, add the butter; Select "sear/sauté" mode and select "md: hi" pressure level.
3. Press "stop/start." After about 4-5 minutes, the butter will start simmering.
4. Add the onion, garlic, and cook (while stirring) until it becomes softened and translucent for 2-3 minutes.
5. Add the turkey, potatoes, and broth; stir gently — season with the ground black pepper and salt.
6. Seal the multi-cooker by locking it with the pressure lid; ensure to keep the pressure release valve locked/sealed.
7. Select "pressure" mode and select the "hi" pressure level. Then, set timer to 10 minutes and press "stop/start"; it will start the cooking process by building up inside pressure.
8. When the timer goes off, quick release pressure by adjusting the pressure valve to the vent. After pressure gets released, open the pressure lid.
9. Select "sear/sauté" mode and select the "md" pressure level; add the cream and vegetables and combine. Stir-cook for 3 minutes to thicken the sauce.
10. In the pie crust, add the cooked mixture and fold the edges. Make a few cuts on top for steam escape.
11. Place the pie crust in the pot.
12. Seal the multi-cooker by locking it with the crisping lid; ensure to keep the pressure release valve locked/sealed.
13. Select "broil" mode and select the "hi" pressure level. Then, set timer to 10 minutes and press "stop/start"; it will start the cooking process by building up inside pressure.
14. When the timer goes off, quick release pressure by adjusting the pressure valve to the vent.
15. After pressure gets released, open the pressure lid.
16. Serve warm and enjoy!

Per Serving: Calories 653, Fats 29g, Carbs 43.5g, Protein 41g

Turkey Dinner Risotto

This is one of the turkey recipes that you should not miss. It is so sweet and spicy! The chicken is made with pepper, lemon and fresh rosemary and is enjoyed by the whole family.

Prep time 10 minutes/ Cook time 15 minutes/ Serves 4
Ingredients:
- 2 boneless turkey breasts, cut into strips
- 2 cups chicken broth
- 1 cup Arborio rice, rinsed, drained
- ¼ cup chopped fresh parsley
- 2 lemons, zested and juiced
- 1 onion, diced
- 2 garlic cloves, minced
- 1 tablespoon dried oregano
- ½ teaspoon sea salt
- 1 ½ tablespoon olive oil
- 8 lemon slices
- Ground black pepper

Directions:
1. Protein: 47g in a zip-lock bag, add the turkey along with the garlic, oregano, sea salt, juice and zest of two lemons.
2. Shake well to combine and set aside to marinate for 20 minutes.
3. Take Ninja Foodi multi-cooker, arrange it over a cooking platform, and open the top lid.
4. In the pot, add the oil; Select "sear/sauté" mode and select "md: hi" pressure level.
5. Press "stop/start." After about 4-5 minutes, the oil will start simmering.
6. Add the onions and cook (while stirring) for 2-3 minutes until they become softened and translucent.
7. Add the rice and chicken broth; season with black pepper and salt to taste.
8. Add the turkey and marinade mixture; stir the mixture.
9. Seal the multi-cooker by locking it with the pressure lid; ensure to keep the pressure release valve locked/sealed.
10. Select "PRESSURE" mode and select the "hi" pressure level. Then, set timer to 12 minutes and press "stop/start"; it will start the cooking process by building up inside pressure.
11. When the timer goes off, quick release pressure by adjusting the pressure valve to the vent. After pressure gets released, open the pressure lid.
12. Serve warm with some lemon slices and enjoy!

Per Serving: Calories: 518, Fats 7g, Carbs 29g, Protein 47g

Italian Turkey Roast

This Italian Turkey Roast is filled with lots of nutrients such as low carbs, fiber, fat, and good protein which help keep you satisfied all day! If you do not train frequently, this is your much-needed diet as it has many nutrients.

Prep time 10 minutes/ Cook time 50 minutes/ Serves 6
Ingredients:
- 1 teaspoon paprika

- 1 teaspoon Italian seasoning
- 1 turkey breasts, with skin
- ¼ cup butter, melted
- 1 clove garlic, minced
- ½ teaspoon herb seasoning blend
- Salt and ground black pepper to taste
- 1 teaspoon shallot, minced

Directions:
1. In a safe microwave bowl, add the butter, garlic, shallot, and other seasonings and shallot. Microwave for 1 minute. Coat the turkey with half the butter mixture.
2. Take Ninja Foodi Grill, arrange it over your kitchen platform, and open the top lid. Lightly grease cooking pot with some oil or cooking spray.
3. Press "roast" and adjust the temperature to 400°F. Adjust the timer to 25 minutes and then press "start/stop." Ninja Foodi will start preheating.
4. Ninja Foodi is preheated and ready to cook when it starts to beep. After you hear a beep, open the top lid.
5. Arrange the turkey directly inside the pot. Close the top lid and allow it to cook until the timer reads zero.
6. Open the lid and brush the turkey with remaining butter. Close the top lid and allow it to cook until the timer reads zero.
7. Open the lid and brush the turkey with remaining butter.
8. Press "roast" and adjust the temperature to 390°F. Adjust the timer to 10 minutes and then press "start/stop."
9. Close the top lid and allow it to cook until the timer reads zero. Serve warm.

Per Serving: Calories 402, Fats 13.5g, Carbs 9g, Protein 56.5g

Funky-Garlic And turkey Breasts

This recipe combines the sweet taste of turkey breasts and the amazing garlic which gives such a delicious outcome.

Prep time 10 minutes/ Cook time 17 minutes/ Serves 4

Ingredients
- ½ teaspoon garlic powder
- 4 tablespoons butter
- ¼ teaspoon dried oregano
- 1-pound turkey breasts, boneless
- 1 teaspoon pepper
- ½ teaspoon salt
- ¼ teaspoon dried basil

Directions
1. Season turkey on both sides generously with garlic, dried oregano, dried basil, salt and pepper
2. Set your Ninja Foodi to sauté mode and add butter, let the butter melt
3. Add turkey breasts and sauté for 2 minutes on each side
4. Lock the lid and select the "Bake/Roast" setting, bake for 15 minutes at 355 degrees F
5. Serve and enjoy once done!

Per Serving: Calories 223, Fats 13g, Carbs 5g, Protein 19g

CHAPTER 4: FISH RECIPES

Salmon Stew

What better way to eat salmon than in a stew? A nutrient-packed stew that you can have with croutons to be filling. Salmon taste good in this delicious sauce, and you will have it over and over again.

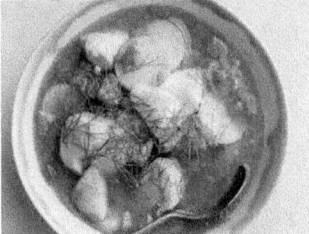

Prep time 10 minutes/ Cook time 11 minutes/ Serves 3
Ingredients:
- 1 cup homemade fish broth
- Salt and black pepper, to taste
- 1 medium onion, chopped
- 1-pound salmon fillet, cubed
- 1 tablespoon butter

Directions
1. Season salmon with salt and pepper.
2. Turn on the Ninja Foodi and select sauté.
3. Add butter, onions and sauté for 3 minutes.
4. Add salmon and fish broth.
5. Close the lid and select "pressure."
6. Set a timer for 8 minutes and do a natural release.
7. Dish out and serve.

Per Serving: Calories 272, Fats 14.2 g, Carbs 4.4 g, Protein 32.1 g

Paprika Shrimp

This hearty dish can be taken at any time and any period, it never goes out of season. It is very easy to cook, and it takes less than half an hour to make.

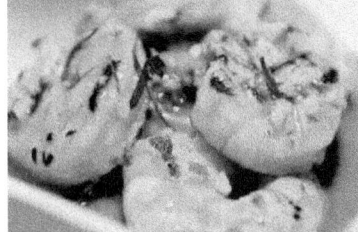

Prep time 10 minutes/ Cook time 15 minutes/ Serves 3
Ingredients:
- 1 teaspoon smoked paprika
- 3 tablespoons butter
- 1-pound tiger shrimps
- Salt

Directions
1. Take a bowl and season shrimps with paprika and salt.
2. Grease pot of Ninja Foodi and add butter in it.
3. Add seasoned shrimps and press "bake/roast."
4. Set the timer to 15 minutes at 355 degrees F.
5. Serve and enjoy.

Per Serving: Calories 173, Fats 8.3 g, Carbs 0.1 g, Protein 23.8 g

Butter Fish

This is a super simple dish that will be on your table within minutes; what is more interesting? Nothing.

Prep time 15 minutes/ Cook time 30 minutes/ Serves 3
Ingredients:
- 1-pound salmon fillets
- 2 tablespoons ginger-garlic paste
- 3 green chilies, chopped
- Salt and black pepper
- ¾ cup butter

Directions
1. Season salmon with salt, pepper and ginger garlic paste.
2. Place salmon in Ninja Foodi and top with butter and green chilies.
3. Close the lid.
4. Select "bake/roast" and set the timer for 30 minutes at 360 degrees F.
5. Open the lid, serve and enjoy.

Per Serving: Calories 507, Fats 45.9 g, Carbs 2.4 g, Protein 22.8 g

Delicious Shrimps

The Shrimp recipe is flavorful and full of nutrients. It is also easy and quick to prepare. It is creamy, spicy, tender and is good for dinner.

Prep time 15 minutes/ Cook time 30 minutes/ Serves 3
Ingredients:
- 2 tablespoons butter
- ½ teaspoon smoked paprika
- 1-pound shrimps, peeled and deveined
- Lemongrass stalks
- 1 red chili pepper, seeded, chopped

Directions
1. Take a bowl and mix all ingredients in it except lemongrass.
2. Marinate for 1 hour.
3. Add this mixture in Ninja pot and close the lid.
4. Select "bake/roast" and set the timer to 15 minutes at 345 degrees F.
5. Open the lid and serve with lemongrass.

Per Serving: Calories 251, Fat 10.3 g, Carbs 3 g, Protein 34.6 g

Sweet and Sour Fish

Want to have the best of both worlds? This is the perfect recipe for that. It is sweet that you will forget that it even has the word sour on it.

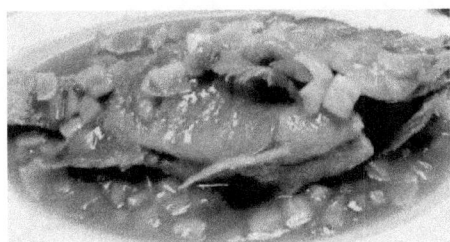

Prep time 15 minutes/ Cook time 6 minutes/ Serves 3
Ingredients:
- 2 drops liquid stevia
- ¼ cup butter
- 1-pound fish chunks
- 1 tablespoon vinegar
- Salt and black pepper

Directions
1. Turn on the Ninja Foodi and select sauté.
2. Add butter, fish and sauté for 3 minutes.
3. Add stevia, vinegar, salt, pepper and select "air crisp."
4. Cook for 3 minutes at 360 degrees F.
5. Serve and enjoy.

Per Serving: Calories 274, Fat 15.4 g, Carbs 2.8 g, Protein 33.2g

Buttery Scallops

Scallops, scallops, scallops! This recipe is given a creamy taste by the butter to make it so amazing.

Prep time 15 minutes/ Cook time 15 minutes/ Serves 6
Ingredients:
- 4 garlic cloves, minced
- 4 tablespoons fresh rosemary, chopped
- 2 pounds sea scallops
- ½ cup butter
- Salt and black pepper

Directions
1. Turn on the Ninja Foodi and select sauté.
2. Add butter, rosemary, garlic and sauté for 1 minute.
3. Add scallops, salt, pepper and sauté for 2 minutes.
4. Select "air crisp" for 3 minutes at 350 degrees F.
5. Dish out and serve.

Per Serving: Calories 279, Fat 16.8 g, Carbs 5.7 g, Protein 25.8 g

Cod with Herbs

Also known as the Pacific Cod, it is a very mild flavored fish and allows all other forms of spices flavor it up just as you will desire.

Prep time 10 minutes/ Cook time 8 minutes/ Serves 6

Ingredients:
- 4 garlic cloves, minced
- 2 teaspoons soy sauce
- ¼ cup butter
- 6 eggs
- 2 small onions, chopped finely
- 3 skinless cod fish fillets, cut into rectangular pieces
- 2 green chilies, chopped finely
- Salt and black pepper

Directions
1. Take a bowl and add all ingredients in it except cod.
2. Mix well and cover each cod fillet in this mixture and set aside.
3. Place trivet in pot and codon a trivet.
4. Lock the lid and select "air crisp."
5. Set the timer to 8 minutes at 330 degrees F.
6. Open the lid, serve and enjoy.

Per Serving: Calories 409, Fat 25.2 g, Carbs 7 g, Protein 37.9 g

Glazed Salmon

Glazed Salmon is one of the best fish on the market to make and passes for a simple dinner or for when you want to impress.

Prep time 10 minutes/ Cook time 13 minutes/ Serves 2

Ingredients:
- 3 tablespoons low sodium soy sauce
- 2 teaspoons lemon juice
- 2 salmon fillets
- 2 teaspoons water

Directions
1. Take a bowl and add all ingredients in it except salmon.
2. Take a small bowl and reserve half of this mixture.
3. Add salmon in the remaining mixture and coat it well.
4. Refrigerate salmon for 2 hours.
5. Turn on the Ninja Foodi and place the trivet in it and salmon on the trivet.
6. Close the lid and select "air crisp."
7. Set the timer to 13 minutes at 355 degrees F.
8. Flip halfway through.
9. Open the lid and serve.

Per Serving: Calories 251, Fat 11.1 g, Carbs 2.4 g, Protein 36 g

Cajun Salmon

Salmon is very good in taste and nutrients. So, in this recipe made to cook in just 15 minutes, I bet you will make it often.

Prep time 15 minutes/ Cook time 23 minutes/ Serves 2
Ingredients:
- 2 tablespoons Cajun seasoning
- 2 salmon fillets

Directions
1. Rub salmon with Cajun seasoning and set it aside.
2. Place salmon on trivet and trivet in the Ninja Foodi.
3. Close the lid and select "air crisp."
4. Select timer to 4 minutes at 390 degrees F.
5. Open the lid and serve.

Per Serving: Calories 235, Fats 11 g, Carbs 0 g, Protein 34.7 g

Spicy Fried Salmon with Avocado Salsa

Salmon has never disappointed when it comes to great taste. Feel free to add a kick of spice to this dish if you will like something hot for the tongue.

Prep time 18 minutes/ Cook time 10 minutes/ Serves 4
Ingredients:
- 5-Ingredients:
- 4 salmon fillets
- 1 large avocado, halved, pitted, and chopped
- 1 small red onion, chopped
- 1 large tomato, deseeded and chopped
- 2 tbsp freshly chopped cilantro
- 1 cup panko breadcrumbs
- ½ tsp cumin powder
- ½ tsp garlic powder
- 1 tsp chili powder
- 1 tsp smoked paprika
- 1 tsp salt
- ¼ tsp freshly ground black pepper
- 1 tbsp apple cider vinegar

Directions
1. Fix the Reversible Rack into the inner pot in the upper position.
2. Close the Air Crisping Lid; select Air Crisp, set the temperature to 390°F, and the time to 5 minutes. Choose Start/Stop to preheat the lid.

3. Meanwhile, in a large zipper bag, add the breadcrumbs, cumin powder, garlic powder, chili powder, paprika, salt, and black pepper. Close the bag and shake well to mix the seasoning.
4. Place the salmon in the bag (two pieces at a time) and shake to coat well with the seasoned crumbs.
5. After the lid has preheated, open and lay the fish on the rack; grease lightly with cooking spray.
6. Close the Air Crisping Lid; select Air Crisp, set the temperature to 390°F, and the time to 10 minutes. Choose Start/Stop to begin cooking the fish and flip halfway of the cooking time.
7. While the fish cooks, in a medium bowl, mix the avocado, onion, tomato, cilantro, and apple cider vinegar.
8. Serve the fish with the salsa when ready.

Per Serving: Calories 506, Fats 21.7g, Carbs 8.8g, Protein 67.09g

Shrimp Bisque

Shrimp Bisques is an ideal seafood recipe to psych you up. It is thick, yummy and very nutritious.

Prep time 15 minutes/ Cook time 15 minutes/ Serves 4

Ingredients:
- 5-Ingredients:
- 2 medium carrots, peeled, chopped
- 2 celery stalks, chopped
- ½ cup diced tomatoes
- 1 ½ cups medium shrimp, peeled, deveined, chopped
- 1 cup heavy cream
- 1 tbsp butter
- 1 small red onion, chopped
- 2 garlic cloves, minced
- 2 ½ cup chicken broth
- 1 tsp old Bay seasoning
- Salt and freshly ground black pepper
- 5 tsp paprika
- 1 tsp dried dill

Directions
1. Select Sear/Sauté on the pot and set to Medium High. Choose Start/Stop to preheat the pot for 5 minutes.
2. Melt the butter in the inner pot and sauté the carrots, celery, and onion until softened, 3 minutes. Mix in the garlic and cook until fragrant, 30 seconds.
3. Stir in the tomatoes, chicken broth, Old Bay seasoning, salt, black pepper, paprika, dill, and shrimp.
4. Cover with the Pressure Lid and lock the vent to Seal. Select Pressure, adjust to High, and set the time to 10 minutes. Select Start/Stop to begin cooking.
5. When done cooking, perform a quick pressure release and carefully open the Pressure Lid.
6. Use a slotted spoon to fetch out the shrimp onto a plate and set aside.
7. Using an immersion blender, puree the soup until smooth and mix in the heavy cream.
8. Spoon the soup into serving bowls and top with the shrimp.
9. Serve warm with bread.

Per Serving: Calories 177, Fats 14.84g, Carbs 9.53g, Protein 3.24g

Fried Scallops in Cilantro Sauce

Hanging with your special someone soon? Make this simple seafood to prove your culinary skills. It is so fast in the making, but the pleasant turn out looks better than the time put it.

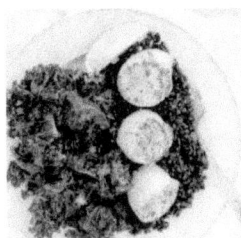

Prep time 15 minutes/ Cook time 5 minutes/ Serves 4

Ingredients:
- 2 cups fresh cilantro leaves
- 1 lemon, zested and juiced
- 3 tbsp heavy cream
- 1 lb. scallops, tendons removed
- 2 tbsp unsalted butter
- 4 garlic cloves, minced
- 1 tbsp Dijon mustard
- Salt and freshly ground black pepper
- ½ cup chicken broth
- 2 tbsp olive oil

Directions
1. Select Sear/Sauté on the pot and set to Medium High. Choose Start/Stop to preheat the pot for 5 minutes.
2. Melt the butter in the inner pot and stir in the cilantro and garlic. Cook until fragrant, 30 seconds. Mix in the lemon zest, lemon juice, Dijon mustard, salt, black pepper, and chicken broth.
3. Cover with the Pressure Lid and lock the vent to Seal. Select Pressure, set to High and set the time to 2 minutes. Choose Start/Stop to begin cooking.
4. After cooking, perform a quick pressure release and open the lid. Then, use an immersion blender to puree the ingredients until smooth.
5. Fix the Reversible Rack over the sauce in the upper position. Season the scallops with salt, black pepper, and arrange on the rack in a single layer; brush with the butter.
6. Close the Air Crisping Lid; select Air Crisp, set the temperature to 390°F, and the time to 2 minutes. Choose Start/Stop to begin cooking the scallops.
7. After 1 minute, open the lid and turn the scallops. Brush with a little more butter and continue cooking with the lid closed.
8. After the timer ends, open the lid and plate the scallops. Remove the rack and top the food with the sauce.
9. Serve warm.

Per Serving: Calories 225, Fats 15.61g, Carbs 6.4g, Protein 14.89g

Breaded Trout with Parsley Pesto

This is one of the recipes that if you have it for the first time, it will be the beginning of your love for it. Try it and see!

Prep time 15 minutes/ Cook time 10 minutes/ Serves 4

Ingredients:
- 4 trout fillets
- 1 lemon, juiced

- 2 cups fresh parsley leaves
- 2 tbsp toasted pine nuts
- 3 tbsp grated Parmesan cheese
- 1 cup panko breadcrumbs
- Salt and freshly ground black pepper to taste
- ¼ tsp dried oregano
- 1 tsp lemon pepper
- 2 garlic cloves, minced
- Salt to taste
- ¼ cup olive oil

Directions
1. Fix the Reversible Rack into the inner pot in the upper position.
2. Close the Air Crisping Lid; select Air Crisp, set the temperature to 390°F, and the time to 5 minutes. Choose Start/Stop to preheat the lid.
3. Meanwhile, in a large zipper bag, add the breadcrumbs, salt, black pepper, and oregano. Close the bag and shake well to mix the seasoning.
4. Place the fish in the bag (two pieces at a time) and shake to coat well with the seasoned crumbs. Remove the fish onto a plate and season both sides with the lemon pepper.
5. After the lid has preheated, open and lay the fish on the rack in a single layer; grease lightly with cooking spray.
6. Close the Air Crisping Lid; select Air Crisp, set the temperature to 390°F, and the time to 10 minutes. Choose Start/Stop to begin cooking the fish and flip halfway of the cooking time.
7. While the fish cooks, in a food processor, combine the parsley, garlic, pine nuts, Parmesan cheese, salt, and olive oil. Blend until smooth.
8. Plate the fish when ready and top with some pesto to taste.
9. Serve immediately.

Per Serving: Calories 402, Fats 30.19g, Carbs 12.52g, Protein 21.89g

Paprika Tuna Cakes

These are a great way to start your day! They will keep you energized for the rest of the day.

Prep time 15 minutes/ Cook time 27 minutes/ Serves 4

Ingredients:
- 2 medium potatoes, peeled, chopped
- 4 cans tuna in oil, drained
- 1 scallion, chopped
- 1 egg, beaten
- 1 tbsp freshly chopped dill
- 1 tsp cayenne pepper
- 4 tbsp plain flour
- Salt and freshly ground black pepper

Directions
1. Pour 1 cup of water with the potatoes into the inner pot.
2. Cover with the Pressure Lid and lock the vent to Seal. Select Pressure, adjust to High, and set the time to 12 minutes. Select Start/Stop to begin cooking.
3. After cooking, perform a quick pressure release and carefully open the lid.
4. Drain the potatoes through a colander, transfer to a large bowl, and clean the inner pot.
5. Place the Cook & Crisp Basket in the inner pot and close the Air Crisping Lid. Select Air Crisp, set the temperature to 375°F, and the time to 5 minutes. Select Start/Stop to preheat the pot.

6.   Meanwhile, add to the potatoes the tuna, scallion, egg, dill, cayenne pepper, flour, salt, and black pepper. Use a potato masher to blend the ingredients and use your hands to form 4 large patties from the mixture.
7.   Arrange the patties in the basket in a single layer and grease lightly with cooking spray.
8.   Close the Air Crisping Lid. Select Air Crisp, set the temperature to 390°F, and the time to 10 minutes. Press Start/Stop to begin baking.
9.   Halfway through the cook time, turn the fish cakes and continue cooking until the time reads to the end.
10.   Transfer to serving plates when ready and serve warm.

Per Serving: Calories 669, Fats 20.34g, Carbs 40.06g, Protein 77.74g

Red Wine Poached Salmon

How about some salmon for dinner or lunch? Sounds like a great idea, right? This recipe is made to set your mood up for the rest of the day's work.

Prep time 15 minutes/ Cook time 11 minutes/ Serves 4

Ingredients:
- 2 celery stalks, chopped
- 5 thyme sprigs
- 4 salmon fillets
- 2 tbsp freshly chopped parsley to garnish
- 2 tbsp red wine vinegar
- 2 cups dry red wine
- 1 cup water
- 1 tbsp sugar
- Salt and freshly ground black pepper

Directions
1.   In the inner pot, mix the celery, thyme, vinegar, red wine, water, sugar, salt, and black pepper. Place the fish in the liquid.
2.   Cover with the Pressure Lid and lock the vent to Seal. Select Steam, adjust to High, and set the time to 3 minutes. Select Start/Stop to begin cooking.
3.   After cooking, perform a quick pressure release and carefully open the lid.
4.   Use tongs, to carefully remove the fish onto serving plates and set aside.
5.   Select Sear/Sauté on the pot and set to Medium High. Choose Start/Stop to continue cooking the sauce until thickened, 5 to 8 minutes.
6.   Spoon the sauce over the salmon, garnish with the parsley and serve warm.

Per Serving: Calories 441, Fats 14.07g, Carbs 3.44g, Protein 65.52g

Garlic Lemon Shrimp with Asparagus

The garlic and lemon give the shrimp an amazing taste that will leave you wanting for more.

Prep time 15 minutes/ Cook time 4 minutes/ Serves 4

Ingredients:
- 1 cup chopped asparagus

- ½ lemon, juiced
- 1 lb. jumbo shrimp, peeled, deveined
- 2 tbsp freshly chopped parsley
- Items from your pantry:
- 1/3 cup butter, divided
- 4 garlic cloves, minced
- Salt and freshly ground black pepper
- ¼ tsp seafood seasoning
- ½ cup chicken broth

Directions
1. Select Sear/Sauté on the pot and set to Medium High. Choose Start/Stop to preheat the pot for 5 minutes.
2. Melt 4 tbsp of the butter in the inner pot and sauté the asparagus for 5 minutes until slightly softened. Mix in the garlic, season with salt and black pepper and cook until fragrant, 30 seconds.
3. Stir in the lemon juice, seafood seasoning, chicken broth, and place in the shrimp. Spoon the sauce to coat the shrimp.
4. Cover with the Pressure Lid and lock the vent to Seal. Select Pressure, set to High and set the time to 3 minutes. Choose Start/Stop to begin cooking.
5. After cooking, perform a quick pressure release until all the steam is out and open the lid.
6. Stir in the parsley, remaining butter and dish the food.

Per Serving: Calories 309, Fats 18.89g, Carbs 3.17g, Protein 30.81g

Tuna in Mango Sauce

Making this recipe in the Ninja Pot is rewarding, so you get to save a lot of time for your work deadlines.

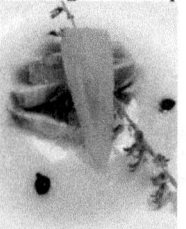

Prep time 15 minutes/ Cook time 5 minutes/ Serves 4

Ingredients:
- 1 cup chopped ripe mangoes
- 1 cup fresh mango juice
- 2 tsp freshly chopped basil
- 4 tuna fillets
- 2 tsp freshly chopped parsley
- 2 tbsp butter
- 1 tbsp apple cider vinegar
- 1 tsp fresh ginger paste
- 1 medium red onion, finely chopped
- ¼ tsp red chili flakes
- Salt and freshly ground black pepper to taste

Directions
1. Select Sear/Sauté on the pot and set to Medium High. Choose Start/Stop to preheat the pot for 5 minutes.
2. Melt the butter in the inner pot and mix in the mangoes, mango juice, basil, vinegar, ginger, onion, and red chili flakes.
3. Cover with the Pressure Lid and lock the vent to Seal. Select Pressure, set to High and set the time to 2 minutes. Choose Start/Stop to begin cooking.
4. After cooking, perform a quick pressure release and open the lid.
5. Fix the Reversible Rack over the sauce in the upper position. Season the tuna with salt, black pepper, and arrange in the rack in a single layer; grease with cooking spray.

6. Close the Air Crisping Lid; select Air Crisp, set the temperature to 390°F, and the time to 3 minutes. Choose Start/Stop to begin cooking the fish.
7. After 2 minutes, open the lid and turn the fish. Coat with a little more oil and continue cooking with the lid closed.
8. After the timer ends, open the lid and plate the tuna. Remove the rack and top the fish with the mango sauce.
9. Garnish with the parsley and serve warm.
Per Serving: Calories 519, Fats 20.14g, Carbs 15.75g, Protein 66.36g

Cod Topped with Mediterranean-Spiced Tomatoes

This recipe is filled with lots of nutrients such as low carbs, fiber, fat, and good protein which help keep you satisfied all day!

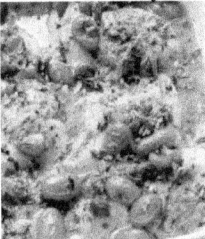

Prep time 5 minutes/ Cook time 10 minutes/ Serves 6
Ingredients:
- 2 frozen or fresh cod fillet
- 1 tablespoon butter
- ½ lemon, juiced
- ½ small onion, sliced thinly
- ¼ teaspoon salt
- ¼ teaspoon black pepper
- ½ teaspoon oregano
- ¼ tsp cumin
- ¼ tsp rosemary
- 4 roma tomatoes, diced
- ¼ cup water

Directions
1. Press sauté and melt butter. Stir in lemon juice, onion, salt, black pepper, oregano cumin, rosemary, and diced tomatoes. Cook for 8 minutes.
2. Add fish and spoon sauce over it. Add water and press stop.
3. Install pressure lid and place valve to vent position.
4. Close Ninja Foodi, press steam button, and set time to 2 minutes.
5. Once done cooking, do a quick release. Serve and enjoy.
Per Serving: Calories 184, carbs 10.0g, protein 20.7g, fats 6.8g

Tilapia Filet Topped with Mango-Salsa

What better way to eat tilapia than with a Mango-Salsa? A nutrient-packed meal that you can have with croutons to be filling.

Prep time 2 minutes/ Cook time 5 minutes/ Serves 2
Ingredients:

- 1 cup coconut milk
- ½ to 1 tablespoon Thai green curry paste
- 1 tablespoon fish sauce
- Zest of 1 lime and juice of ½ lime
- 2 teaspoons sear button sugar
- 1 teaspoon garlic, minced
- 1 tablespoon fresh ginger, minced
- 2 6-oz Tilapia filet
- 1 lime, cut in thin slices
- A sprinkle of cilantro leaves and chopped scallion
- 1 mango, peeled, seeded, and diced
- 1 Fresno or jalapeno chiles, minced
- 1 scallion, finely chopped
- A handful of cilantro leaves, chopped
- Juice, 1 lime

Directions
1. In a bowl, mix well coconut milk, Thai green curry paste, fish sauce, lime juice, lime zest, sear button sugar, garlic, and ginger. Add fish and marinate for at least an hour.
2. Meanwhile, make the mango salsa by combining all ingredients in a separate bowl. Keep in the fridge.
3. Cut two 11x11-inch foil. Place one fish fillet in each foil. Top each equally with lime, scallion and cilantro. Seal foil packets.
4. Add a cup of water in Ninja Foodi, place trivet, and add foil packets on trivet.
5. Install pressure lid.
6. Close Ninja Foodi, press pressure button, choose high settings, and set time to 5 minutes.
7. Once done cooking, do a quick release.
8. Serve and enjoy with mango salsa on top.

Per Serving: Calories 372, carbs 28.5g, protein 29.3g, fats 15.6g

Coconut Curry Sea Bass

Luxury in one pot is what this recipe is. It is rich in nutrients. For someone who is crazy about seafood, they will easily make it their go-to any day and I think you will love it the same way, if not more.

Prep time 2 minutes/ Cook time 3 minutes/ Serves 2

Ingredients:
- 1 can coconut milk
- Juice, 1 lime
- 1 tablespoon red curry paste
- 1 teaspoon fish sauce
- 1 teaspoon coconut aminos
- 1 teaspoon honey
- 2 teaspoons sriracha
- 2 cloves garlic, minced
- 1 teaspoon ground turmeric
- 1 teaspoon ground ginger
- ½ teaspoon sea salt
- ½ teaspoon white pepper
- 1-pound sea bass, cut into 1" cubes
- ¼ cup chopped fresh cilantro

- 2 lime wedges

Directions
1. Whisk well pepper, salt, ginger, turmeric, garlic, sriracha, honey, coconut aminos, fish sauce, red curry paste, lime juice, and coconut milk in a large bowl.
2. Place fish in pot and pour coconut milk mixture over it.
3. Install pressure lid. Close Ninja Foodi, press pressure button, choose high settings, and set time to 3 minutes.
4. Once done cooking, do a quick release.
5. Serve and enjoy with equal amounts of lime wedge and cilantro.

Per Serving: Calories 749, carbs 16.6g, protein 58.0g, fats 50.0g

Tomato-Basil Dressed Tilapia

The tomatoes give the Tilapia a thick look and a great taste. You cannot fail to love this great meal.

Prep time 2 minutes/ Cook time 4 minutes/ Serves 2

Ingredients:
- 2 tilapia fillets
- Salt and pepper
- 2 roma tomatoes, diced
- 2 minced garlic cloves
- ¼ cup chopped basil, fresh
- 1 tbsp olive oil
- ¼ tsp salt
- 1/8 tsp pepper
- 1 tbsp Balsamic vinegar

Directions
1. Add a cup of water in Ninja Foodi, place steamer basket, and add tilapia in basket. Season with pepper and salt.
2. Install pressure lid and place valve to vent position.
3. Close Ninja Foodi, press steam button, and set time to 2 minutes.
4. Meanwhile, in a medium bowl toss well to mix pepper, salt, olive oil, basil, garlic, and tomatoes. If desired, you can add a tablespoon of balsamic vinegar. Mix well.
5. Once done cooking, do a quick release.
6. Serve and enjoy with the basil-tomato dressing.

Per Serving: Calories 196, carbs 2.0g, protein 20.0g, fats 12.0g

Pasta 'n Tuna Bake

Pasta is a favorite for many and with tuna on board, all I can say is that it is simply amazing

Prep time 3 minutes/ Cook time 10 minutes/ Serves 2

Ingredients:

- 1 can cream-of-mushroom soup
- 1 ½ cups water
- 1 ¼ cups macaroni pasta
- 1 can tuna
- ½ cup frozen peas
- ½ tsp salt
- 1 tsp pepper
- ½ cup shredded cheddar cheese

Directions
1. Mix soup and water in Ninja Foodi.
2. Add remaining ingredients except for cheese. Stir.
3. Install pressure lid.
4. Close Ninja Foodi, press pressure button, choose high settings, and set time to 4 minutes.
5. Once done cooking, do a quick release.
6. Remove pressure lid.
7. Stir in cheese and roast for 5 minutes.
8. Serve and enjoy.

Per Serving: Calories 378, carbs 34.0g, protein 28.0g, fats 14.1g

Salmon-Pesto Over Pasta

Salmon and pasta are a long existing recipe but the taste and nutrients derived never disappoint. So, you definitely should make it now and even often.

Prep time 5 minutes/ Cook time 10 minutes/ Serves 2

Ingredients:
- 4 ounces dry pasta
- 1 cup water
- 3-ounces smoked salmon, broken up in bite sized pieces
- ¼ lemon
- Salt and pepper
- ½ teaspoon grated lemon zest
- ½ teaspoon lemon juice
- 2 tbsp heavy cream
- 1 tbsp walnuts
- 1 clove garlic
- 1 cup packed baby spinach
- 1 ½ tbsp olive oil
- ¼ cup freshly grated parmesan + more for serving/garnish
- Kosher salt and black pepper to taste
- 1 tsp grated lemon zest
- ¼ cup heavy cream

Directions
1. Make the sauce in blender by pulsing garlic and walnuts until chopped. Add ¼ tsp pepper, ¼ tsp salt, ½ cup parmesan, oil, and 2/3s of spinach. Puree until smooth.
2. Add butter, water, and pasta in Ninja Foodi.
3. Install pressure lid.
4. Close Ninja Foodi, press pressure button, choose high settings, and set time to 4 minutes.
5. Once done cooking, do a quick release.

6. Press stop and then press sauté.
7. Stir in remaining parmesan, remaining spinach, sauce, lemon juice, lemon zest, heavy cream, and smoked salmon. Mix well and sauté for 5 minutes.
8. Serve and enjoy.

Per Serving: Calories 465, carbs 31.0g, protein 20.1g, fats 29.0g

Sweet 'n Spicy Mahi-Mahi

It is not surprising that a pretty colored fish like this taste great in turn. Mahi-Mahi works well with different spices, ginger, cumin, fruity flavors, sweet sauce, and peppers.

Prep time 4 minutes/ Cook time 10 minutes/ Serves 2

Ingredients:
- 2 6-oz mahi-mahi fillets
- Salt
- Black pepper, to taste
- 1-2 cloves garlic, minced or crushed
- 1" piece ginger, finely grated
- ½ lime, juiced
- 2 tablespoons honey
- 1 tablespoon nanami togarashi
- 2 tablespoons sriracha
- 1 tablespoon orange juice

Directions
1. In a heatproof dish that fits inside the Ninja Foodi, mix well orange juice, sriracha, nanami togarashi, honey lime juice, ginger, and garlic.
2. Season mahi-mahi with pepper and salt. Place in bowl of sauce and cover well in sauce. Seal dish securely with foil.
3. Install pressure lid and place valve to vent position.
4. Add a cup of water in Ninja Foodi, place trivet, and add dish of mahi-mahi on trivet.
5. Close Ninja Foodi, press steam button and set time to 10 minutes.
6. Once done cooking, do a quick release.
7. Serve and enjoy.

Per Serving: Calories 200, carbs 20.1g, protein 28.1g, fats 0.8g

Easy Veggie-Salmon Bake

The Veggie-Salmon Bake recipe is made with veggies and some aromatic spices to set your mood up for the rest of the day's work.

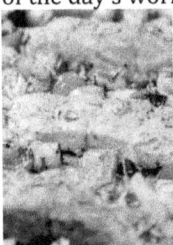

Prep time 5 minutes/ Cook time 20 minutes/ Serves 2

Ingredients:
- 1 cup chicken broth

- 1 cup milk
- 1 salmon filet
- 2 tbsp olive oil
- Ground pepper to taste
- 1 tsp minced garlic
- 1 cup frozen vegetables
- ½ can of cream of celery soup
- ¼ tsp dill
- ¼ tsp cilantro
- 1 tsp Italian spice
- 1 tsp poultry seasoning
- 1 tbsp ground parmesan

Directions
1. Press sauté button and heat oil.
2. Add the salmon and cook until white on both sides and defrosted enough to split apart, around 2 minutes per side.
3. Add the garlic and just stir into the oil then deglaze the pot with the broth for 3 minutes.
4. Add the spices, milk, vegetables, noodles and stir.
5. Add the cream of celery soup on top and just gently stir so it is mixed in enough on top to not be clumpy.
6. Install pressure lid. Close Ninja Foodi, press pressure cook button, choose high settings, and set time to 8 minutes.
7. Once done cooking, do a quick release.
8. Serve and enjoy with a sprinkle of parmesan.

Per Serving: Calories 616, carbs 28.7g, protein 51.8g, fats 32.6g

Salmon with Orange-Ginger Sauce

Salmon is very good in taste and nutrients. So, in this sauce made to cook in just 15 minutes, I bet you will make it often.

Prep time 3 minutes/ Cook time 15 minutes/ Serves 2

Ingredients:
- 1-pound salmon
- 1 tablespoon dark soy sauce
- 2 teaspoons minced ginger
- 1 teaspoon minced garlic
- 1 teaspoon salt
- 1 ½ tsp ground pepper
- 2 tablespoons low sugar marmalade

Directions
1. In a heatproof pan that fits inside your Ninja Foodi, add salmon.
2. Mix all the sauce ingredients and pour over the salmon. Allow to marinate for 15-30 minutes. Cover pan with foil securely.
3. Put 2 cups of water in Ninja Foodi and add trivet.
4. Place the pan of salmon on trivet.
5. Install pressure lid. Close Ninja Foodi, press pressure button, choose low settings, and set time to 5 minutes.
6. Once done cooking, do a quick release.
7. Serve and enjoy.

Per Serving: Calories 177, carbs 8.8g, protein 24.0g, fats 5.0g

Coconut Curry Fish

The turnout for Coconut Curry Fish is dope and I know you will say the same. It also gets ready in just 15 minutes rather than 1 hour that it will usually take on the stove top.

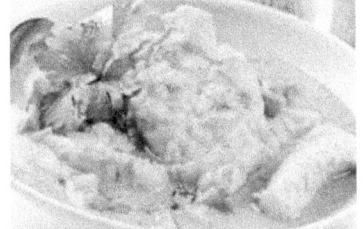

Prep time 5 minutes/ Cook time 15 minutes/ Serves 2

Ingredients:
- 1-lb fish steaks or fillets, rinsed and cut into bite-size pieces
- 1 tomato, chopped
- 1 green chiles, sliced into strips
- 1 small onions, sliced into strips
- 2 garlic cloves, squeezed
- ½ tbsp freshly grated ginger
- 2 bay laurel leaves
- 1 tsp ground coriander
- 1 tsp ground cumin
- ½ tsp ground turmeric
- ½ tsp chili powder
- ½ tsp ground fenugreek
- 1 cup unsweetened coconut milk
- Salt to taste

Directions
1. Press sauté button and heat oil. Add garlic, sauté for a minute. Stir in ginger and onions. Sauté for 5 minutes. Stir in bay leaves, fenugreek, chili powder, turmeric, cumin, and coriander. Cook for a minute.
2. Add coconut milk and deglaze pot.
3. Stir in tomatoes and green chilies. Mix well.
4. Add fish and mix well.
5. Install pressure lid and place valve to vent position.
6. Close Ninja Foodi, press pressure cook button, choose low settings, and set time to 5 minutes.
7. Once done cooking, do a quick release.
8. Adjust seasoning to taste.
9. Serve and enjoy.

Per Serving: Calories 434, carbs 11.7g, protein 29.7g, fats 29.8g

Seafood Gumbo New Orleans Style

The sea food gumbo is a great seafood meal. This is a great meal to spice up your day.

Prep time 5 minutes/ Cook time 20 minutes/ Serves 2

Ingredients:
- 1 sea bass filet patted dry and cut into 2" chunks

- 1 tablespoon ghee or avocado oil
- 1 tablespoon Cajun seasoning
- 1 small yellow onion diced
- 1 small bell pepper diced
- 1 celery rib diced
- 2 roma tomatoes diced
- 1 tbsp tomato paste
- 1 bay leaf
- ½ cup bone broth
- ¾-pound medium to large raw shrimp deveined
- Sea salt
- Black pepper

Directions
1. Press sauté button and heat oil.
2. Season fish chunks with pepper, salt, and half of Cajun seasoning. Once oil is hot, sear fish chunks for 3 minutes per side and gently transfer to a plate.
3. Stir in remaining Cajun seasoning, celery, and onions. Sauté for 2 minutes. Press stop.
4. Stir in bone broth, bay leaves, tomato paste, and diced tomatoes. Mix well. Add back fish.
5. Install pressure lid and place valve to vent position.
6. Close Ninja Foodi, press pressure cook button, choose high settings, and set time to 5 minutes.
7. Once done cooking, do a quick release.
8. Stir in shrimps. Cover and let it sit for 5 minutes. Open and mix well.
9. Serve and enjoy.

Per Serving: Calories 357, carbs 14.8g, protein 45.9g, fats 12.6g

Creamy Herb 'n Parm Salmon

Salmon is a very delicious that is loved by almost everyone that has ever tasted it.

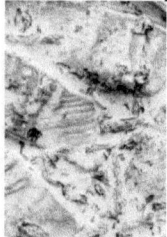

Prep time 3 minutes/ Cook time 10 minutes/ Serves 2

Ingredients:
- 2 frozen salmon filets
- ½ cup water
- 1 ½ tsp minced garlic
- ¼ cup heavy cream
- 1 cup parmesan cheese grated
- 1 tbsp chopped fresh chives
- 1 tbsp chopped fresh parsley
- 1 tbsp fresh dill
- 1 tsp fresh lemon juice
- Salt and pepper to taste

Directions
1. Add water and trivet in pot. Place fillets on top of trivet.
2. Install pressure lid. Close Ninja Foodi, press pressure button, choose high settings, and set time to 4 minutes.
3. Once done cooking, do a quick release.
4. Transfer salmon to a serving plate. And remove trivet.

5. Press stop and then press sauté button on Ninja Foodi. Stir in heavy cream once water begins to boil. Boil for 3 minutes. Press stop and then stir in lemon juice, parmesan cheese, dill, parsley, and chives. Season with pepper and salt to taste. Pour over salmon.
6. Serve and enjoy.
Per Serving: Calories 423, carbs 6.4g, protein 43.1g, fats 25.0g

Stewed Mixed Seafood

This recipe is very easy to cook, and it takes about half an hour to make, and your seafood stew would be in front of you.

Prep time 5 minutes/ Cook time 35 minutes/ Serves 2
Ingredients:
- 1 tbsp vegetable oil
- ½ 14.5-oz can fire-roasted tomatoes
- ½ cup diced onion
- ½ cup chopped carrots, or 1 cup chopped bell pepper
- ½ cup water
- ½ cup white wine or broth
- 1 bay leaf
- ½ tablespoon tomato paste
- 1 tablespoon minced garlic
- 1 teaspoon fennel seeds toasted and ground
- ½ teaspoon dried oregano
- 1 teaspoon salt
- 1 teaspoon red pepper flakes
- 2 cups mixed seafood such as fish chunks, shrimp, bay scallops, mussels and calamari rings, defrosted
- 1 tablespoon fresh lemon juice

Directions
1. Press sauté button on Ninja Foodi and heat oil. Once hot, stir in onion and garlic. Sauté for 5 minutes. Stir in tomatoes, bay leaves, tomato paste, oregano, salt, and pepper flakes. Cook for 5 minutes. Press stop.
2. Stir in bell pepper, water, wine, and fennel seeds. Mix well.
3. Install pressure lid. Close Ninja Foodi, press pressure button, choose high settings, and set time to 15 minutes.
4. Once done cooking, do a quick release.
5. Stir in defrosted mixed seafood. Cover and let it cook for 10 minutes in residual heat.
6. Serve and enjoy with a dash of lemon juice.
Per Serving: Calories 202, carbs 10.0g, protein 18.0g, fats 10.0g

CHAPTER 5: BEEF RECIPES

Beef 'n Mushrooms in Thick Sauce

Beef and Mushrooms are a long existing recipe but the taste and nutrients derived never disappoint. So, you definitely should make it many times.

Prep time 5 minutes/ Cook time 30 minutes/ Serves 2
Ingredients:
- ½ tablespoon butter
- ½ pound beef chunks
- Salt and pepper to taste
- ½ cup onions, chopped
- ½ tablespoon garlic, minced
- 1 carrot, sliced diagonally
- ¼ cup chopped celery
- 1/3 cup mushrooms, halved
- 1 medium potato, peeled and quartered
- 1 tablespoon Worcestershire sauce
- 1 tablespoon tomato paste
- ½ cup chicken broth
- 1 tablespoon all-purpose flour + 1 tablespoon water

Directions:
1. Turn on the sauté button on the Ninja Foodi and melt the butter. Sear button the beef chunks and season with salt and pepper to taste. Add the onions and garlic until fragrant.
2. Stir in the carrots, celery, mushrooms and potatoes.
3. Add the Worcestershire sauce, tomato paste, and chicken broth. Season with more salt and pepper to taste.
4. Install pressure lid. Close Ninja Foodi, press the pressure button, choose high settings, and set time to 30 minutes.
5. Once done cooking, do a quick release.
6. Open the lid and press the sauté button. Stir in the all-purpose flour and allow to simmer until the sauce thickens.
7. Serve and enjoy.

Per Serving: Calories 539; carbohydrates: 61.3g; protein 43.9g, fat: 13.1g

Beef Stew Recipe from Ethiopia

This beef stew is a given when it comes to making awesome stews. The ingredients cook faster in this case especially the beef which cooks so soft to tear apart as you dig your spoon in.

Prep time 6 minutes/ Cook time 55 minutes/ Serves 2
Ingredients:

- 1-pound beef stew meat, cut into chunks
- ¼ teaspoon turmeric powder
- 1 tablespoon garam masala
- 1 tablespoon coriander powder
- 1 teaspoon cumin
- ¼ teaspoon ground nutmeg
- 2 teaspoons smoked paprika
- ¼ teaspoon black pepper
- 2 tablespoons ghee
- 1 onion, chopped
- 1 tablespoon ginger, grated
- 2 cloves of garlic, grated
- 1 tablespoon onions
- 3 tablespoons tomato paste
- ½ teaspoon sugar
- Salt and pepper to taste
- 1 cup water

Directions:
1. In a mixing bowl, combine the first 8 ingredients and allow to marinate in the fridge for at least 4 hours.
2. Press the sauté button and heat the oil. Sauté the onion, ginger, and garlic until fragrant. Stir in the marinated beef and allow to sear button for 3 minutes.
3. Stir in the rest of the ingredients.
4. Install pressure lid. Close Ninja Foodi, press the pressure button, choose high settings, and set time to 50 minutes.
5. Once done cooking, do a quick release.
6. Serve and enjoy.

Per serving: Calories 591; carbohydrates: 11.5g; protein: 83.5g; fat: 23.4g

Beef Cooked in Mango-Turmeric Spice

Beef recipes never disappoint and so is this one. Enjoy this stew with the family at dinner; they'll love you without fail.

Prep time 4 minutes/ Cook time 50 minutes/ Serves 2

Ingredients:
- 1-pound beef shin, cut into chunks
- ½ teaspoon ground cinnamon
- ¼ teaspoon ground cloves
- 1 teaspoon dried mango powder
- 1 teaspoon ground turmeric
- ½ teaspoon ground cumin
- 3 cloves of garlic, minced
- 1 tablespoon lemon juice
- 1 teaspoon honey
- 12 cardamom pods, bashed
- Salt and pepper to taste
- 2 tablespoons ghee
- 1 cup onions, cut into wedges
- 2 green chilies, sliced

- 2 tomatoes, chopped
- 1 cup water

Directions:
1. In a mixing bowl, combine the first 11 ingredients and allow to marinate in the fridge for at least 2 hours.
2. Press the sauté button on the Ninja Foodi and add the ghee. Stir in the marinated beef and sear button on all sides for at least 5 minutes.
3. Stir in the rest of the ingredients.
4. Install pressure lid. Close Ninja Foodi, press the pressure button, choose high settings, and set time to 45 minutes.
5. Once done cooking, do a quick release.
6. Serve and enjoy.

Per serving: Calories 463; carbohydrates: 19.3g; protein: 51.5g; fat: 20g

St. Patty's Corned Beef Recipe

This dish goes well with a side of steamed asparagus and you may have a hot sauce on the side to kick things up.

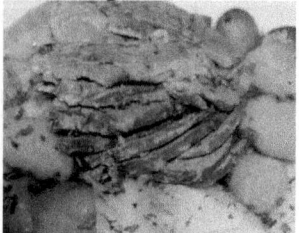

Prep time 6 minutes/ Cook time 60 minutes/ Serves 2

Ingredients:
- 2 cloves of garlic, chopped
- ½ onion, quartered
- 1 ¼ pounds corned beef brisket, cut in large slices
- 3-oz. Beer
- 1 cup water
- 2 small carrots, roughly chopped
- 1 small potato, chopped
- ½ head cabbage, cut into four pieces

Directions:
1. In the Ninja Foodi, place the garlic, onion, corned beef brisket, beer, and water. Season with salt and pepper to taste.
2. Install pressure lid. Close Ninja Foodi, press the pressure button, choose high settings, and set time to 50 minutes.
3. Once done cooking, do a quick release. Open the lid and take out the meat. Shred the meat using fork and place it back into the Ninja Foodi.
4. Stir in the vegetables.
5. Install pressure lid. Close the lid and seal the vent and press the pressure button. Cook for another 10 minutes. Do quick release.

Per serving: Calories 758; carbohydrates: 45.8g; protein: 43.1g; fat: 44.7g

Potatoes, Beefy-Cheesy Way

Having a Ninja Pot without making this recipe is not permissible. You need to make this once and many times for yourself and your guests.

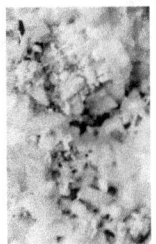

Prep time 5 minutes/ Cook time 25 minutes/ Serves 2
Ingredients:
- ½ pounds ground beef
- 2 large potatoes, peeled and chopped
- ¾ cup cheddar cheese, shredded
- ¼ cup chicken broth
- ½ tablespoon Italian seasoning mix
- Salt and pepper to taste

Directions:
1. Press the sauté button on the Ninja Foodi and stir in the beef. Sear button the meat until some of the oil has rendered.
2. Add the rest of the ingredients.
3. Install pressure lid.
4. Close Ninja Foodi, press the pressure button, choose high settings, and set time to 20 minutes.
5. Once done cooking, do a quick release.

Per serving: Calories 801; carbohydrates: 66.8g; protein: 53.4g; fat: 35.6g

Beef Pot Pie

With an ultimate dish like this on the table, you needn't yell to get everyone around. It smells so good and tastes fantastic. Make a good choice of beef, trim off any excess fat with a knife, and head up to begin cooking.

Prep time 6 minutes/ Cook time 25 minutes/ Serves 2
Ingredients:
- 1 ½ tablespoons butter
- ½ cup diced onion
- ½ cup diced celery
- 2 cloves of garlic, minced
- 6-oz beef
- 1 teaspoon dried thyme
- ¾ cup potatoes, diced
- 1/3 cup carrots, diced
- 1/3 cup frozen peas
- ¾ cups beef broth
- 2 tbsp milk
- 1 tablespoon cornstarch + 1 ½ tablespoons water
- ½ box puff pastry
- 1 egg white

Directions:
1. Press the sauté button on the Ninja Foodi and heat the butter. Sauté the onion, celery and garlic until fragrant. Add the beef and sear button for 5 minutes.

2. Stir in the thyme, potatoes, carrots, frozen peas, beef broth and milk.
3. Install pressure lid. Close Ninja Foodi, press pressure button, choose high settings, and set time to 10 minutes.
4. Once done cooking, do a quick release.
5. Ladle into two ramekins and cover the top of the ramekins with puff pastry. Brush the top with egg whites.
6. Place in Ninja Foodi, bake at 3500F for 10 minutes or until tops are lightly browned.

Per serving: Calories 328; carbohydrates: 26.6g; protein: 20.8g; fat: 15.3g

Healthy 'n Tasty Meatloaf

However, the wait when cooking is rewarded with a very delicious meal that is so tasty! The chance of messing up on meatloaf is close to zero; a reason that makes it a favorite for many! To spice it up add up carrots, zucchini, bell peppers etc.

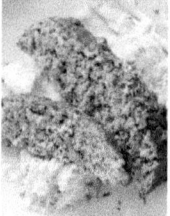

Prep time 7 minutes/ Cook time 20 minutes/ Serves 2

Ingredients:
- ¾-pound ground beef
- ¾ cup bread crumbs
- 1/3 cup parmesan cheese
- 2 small eggs, beaten
- 1 tablespoon minced garlic
- 1 teaspoon steak seasoning
- Salt and pepper to taste
- 1 ½ teaspoons sear button sugar
- ¼ cup ketchup
- ½ tablespoon mustard
- 1 teaspoon Worcestershire sauce

Directions:
1. Place a trivet in the Ninja Foodi and pour a cup of beef broth.
2. In a mixing bowl, mix together the beef, bread crumbs, cheese, eggs, garlic, and steak seasoning. Season with salt and pepper to taste.
3. Pour meat mixture in a heat-proof pan and place on top of the trivet. Cover top with foil.
4. Install pressure lid. Close Ninja Foodi, press the steam button, and set time to 20 minutes.
5. While waiting for the meatloaf to cook, combine in a saucepan the sugar, ketchup, mustard, and Worcestershire sauce. Mix until the sauce becomes thick.
6. Once done cooking, do a quick release.
7. Remove the meatloaf from the Ninja Foodi and allow to cool.
8. Serve with sauce and enjoy.

Per serving: Calories 574; carbohydrates: 23.2g; protein: 46.6g; fat: 32.7g

Beefy Stew Recipe from Persia

With love from Persia, this beef stew is so rich in flavors that you will not want to just make it once.

Prep time 6 minutes/ Cook time 20 minutes/ Serves 2
Ingredients:
- 1 tablespoons vegetable oil
- 1 onion, chopped
- 2 cloves of garlic, minced
- ¾-pound beef stew meat, cut into chunks
- ½ tablespoon ground cumin
- ¼ teaspoon saffron threads
- ½ teaspoon turmeric
- ¼ teaspoon ground cinnamon
- ¼ teaspoon ground allspice
- Salt and pepper to taste
- 2 tbsp tomato paste
- ½ can split peas, rinsed and drained
- 2 cups bone broth
- 1 can crushed tomatoes
- 2 tablespoon lemon juice, freshly squeezed

Directions:
1. Press the sauté button on the Ninja Foodi. Heat the oil and sauté the onion and garlic until fragrant. Add cumin, saffron, turmeric, cinnamon, and allspice. Stir in the beef and sear button for 3 minutes. Season with salt and pepper to taste.
2. Pour in the rest of the ingredients.
3. Install pressure lid. Close Ninja Foodi, press the pressure button, choose high settings, and set time to 20 minutes.
4. Once done cooking, do a quick release.

Per serving: Calories 466; carbohydrates: 36g; protein: 49g; fat: 14g

Bacon-Wrapped Hot Dogs

Whether it is a hot summer afternoon or the middle of winter, with the Ninja Foodi you can crisp these bacon-wrapped hot dogs to perfection in just minutes and enjoy summertime flavors year-round!

Prep time 15 minutes/ Cook time 15 minutes/ Serves 3
- 4 beef hot dogs
- 4 bacon strips
- Cooking spray
- 4 bakery hot dog buns, split and toasted
- ½ red onion, chopped
- 1 cup sauerkraut, rinsed and drained

Directions:

1. Place Cook & Crisp Basket in pot. Close crisping lid. Select AIR CRISP, set temperature to 360°F, and set time to 5 minutes. Select START/STOP to begin preheating.
2. Wrap each hot dog with 1 strip of bacon, securing it with toothpicks as needed.
3. Once unit has preheated, open lid and coat the basket with cooking spray. Place the hot dogs in the basket in a single layer. Close crisping lid.
4. Select AIR CRISP, set temperature to 360°F, and set time to 15 minutes. Select START/STOP to begin.
5. After 10 minutes, open lid and check doneness. If needed, continue cooking until it reaches your desired doneness.
6. When cooking is complete, place the hot dog in the buns with the onion and sauerkraut. Top, if desired, with condiments of your choice, such as yellow mustard, ketchup, or mayonnaise.

Per serving: Calories: 336; Fat: 17g; Carbohydrates: 27g; Protein: 20g

Wholesome Asparagus Beef

This beef recipe is given a tender and smooth look by the asparagus and it's taste is awesome.

Prep time 8 minutes/ Cook time 28 minutes/ Serves 4

Ingredients:
- 1-pound beef stew meat, cut into cubes
- 2 tablespoons grated ginger
- 1 cup tomato puree
- A pinch of black pepper and salt
- ½ pound asparagus, trimmed, steamed and halved
- 1 yellow onion, chopped
- 1 tablespoon olive oil

Directions:
1. Take Ninja Foodi multi-cooker, arrange it over a cooking platform, and open the top lid.
2. In the pot, add the oil; Select "SEAR/SAUTÉ" mode and select "MD: HI" pressure level.
3. Press "STOP/START." After about 4-5 minutes, the oil will start simmering.
4. Add the meat and stir cook for about 5 minutes to brown evenly.
5. Add the onion, ginger, black pepper, and salt; cook, while stirring, for 4 minutes more. Add the tomato puree; stir the mixture.
6. Seal the multi-cooker by locking it with the pressure lid; ensure to keep the pressure release valve locked/sealed.
7. Select "PRESSURE" mode and select the "HI" pressure level. Then, set timer to 15 minutes and press "STOP/START"; it will start the cooking process by building up inside pressure.
8. When the timer goes off, naturally release inside pressure for about 8-10 minutes. Then, quick-release pressure by adjusting the pressure valve to the VENT.
9. After pressure gets released, open the pressure lid.
10. Select "SEAR/SAUTÉ" mode and select the "MD" pressure level; add the asparagus and combine. Stir-cook for 4 minutes.

Per Serving: Calories: 243, Fat: 10.5g, Carbohydrates: 10g, Protein: 35g

Warm and Beefy Meat Loaf

Are you a meatloaf lover? This is beef meatloaf is any meatloaf lover's favorite. For anyone who hasn't tried meatloaf before, this is the ideal recipe to start with.

Prep time 10 minutes/ Cook time 70 minutes/ Serves 6
Ingredients
- ½ cup onion, chopped
- 2 garlic cloves, minced
- ¼ cup sugar free ketchup
- 1 pound grass fed-lean ground beef
- ½ cup green bell pepper, seeded and chopped
- 1 cup cheddar cheese, grated
- 2 organic eggs, beaten
- 1 teaspoon dried thyme, crushed
- 3 cups fresh spinach, chopped
- 6 cups mozzarella cheese, freshly grated
- Black pepper to taste

Directions:
1. Take a bowl and add all of the listed ingredients except cheese and spinach
2. Place a wax paper on a smooth surface and arrange the meat over it
3. Top with spinach, cheese and roll the paper around the paper to form a nice meat loaf
4. Remove wax paper and transfer loaf to your Ninja Foodi
5. Lock lid and select "Bake/Roast" mode, setting the timer to 70 minutes and temperature to 380 degrees F
6. Let it bake and take the dish out once done

Per Serving: Calories: 409, Fat: 16g, Carbohydrates: 5g, Protein: 56g

Wise Corned Beef

This recipe is very easy to make, it takes just one hour to make, and your Corned Beef are ready.

Prep time 10 minutes/ Cook time 60 minutes/ Serves 4
Ingredients
- 4 pounds beef brisket
- 2 garlic cloves, peeled and minced
- 2 yellow onions, peeled and sliced
- 11 ounces celery, thinly sliced
- 1 tablespoon dried dill
- 3 bay leaves
- 4 cinnamon sticks, cut into halves
- Salt and pepper to taste
- 17 ounces water

Directions
1. Take a bowl and add beef, add water and cover, let it soak for 2-3 hours
2. Drain and transfer to the Ninja Foodi

3. Add celery, onions, garlic, bay leaves, dill, cinnamon, dill, salt, pepper and rest of the water to the Ninja Foodi
4. Stir and combine it well
5. Lock lid and cook on HIGH pressure for 50 minutes
6. Release pressure naturally over 10 minutes
7. Transfer meat to cutting board and slice, divide amongst plates and pour the cooking liquid (alongside veggies) over the servings

Per Serving: Calories: 289, Fat: 21g, Carbohydrates: 14g, Protein: 9g

Elegant Beef Curry

You can call it a world passer simply because it works with so many kinds of dishes across continents and can be made just anywhere easily.

Prep time 10 minutes/ Cook time 20 minutes/ Serves 4
Ingredients
- 2 pounds beef steak, cubed
- 2 tablespoons extra virgin olive oil
- 1 tablespoon Dijon mustard
- 2 and ½ tablespoons curry powder
- 2 yellow onions, peeled and chopped
- 2 garlic cloves, peeled and minced
- 10 ounces canned coconut milk
- 2 tablespoons tomato sauce
- Salt and pepper to taste

Directions
1. Set your Ninja Foodi to "Saute" mode and add oil, let it heat up
2. Add onions, garlic, stir cook for 4 minutes
3. Add mustard, stir and cook for 1 minute
4. Add beef and stir until all sides are browned
5. Add curry powder, salt and pepper, stir cook for 2 minutes
6. Add coconut milk and tomato sauce, stir and cove
7. Lock lid and cook on HIGH pressure for 10 minutes
8. Release pressure naturally over 10 minutes

Per Serving: Calories: 275, Fat: 12g, Carbohydrates: 12g, Protein: 27g

Mesmerizing Beef Sirloin Steak

Beef Sirloin Steak is perfect when you want something heavy but easy for lunch or dinner.

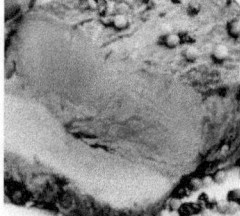

Prep time 5 minutes/ Cook time 17 minutes/ Serves 4
Ingredients
- 3 tablespoons butter

- ½ teaspoon garlic powder
- 1-2 pounds beef sirloin steaks
- Salt and pepper to taste
- 1 garlic clove, minced

Directions
1. Set your Ninja Foodi to sauté mode and add butter, let the butter melt
2. Add beef sirloin steaks
3. Saute for 2 minutes on each side
4. Add garlic powder, garlic clove, salt and pepper
5. Lock lid and cook on Medium-HIGH pressure for 15 minutes
6. Release pressure naturally over 10 minutes
7. Transfer prepare Steaks to serving platter, enjoy!

Per Serving: Calories: 246, Fat: 13g, Carbohydrates: 2g, Protein: 31g

Epic Beef Sausage Soup

Remember to make this soup as a saver for the cold nights. You can add a shake of hot sauce to it but most importantly, serve it warm to have the best satisfaction.

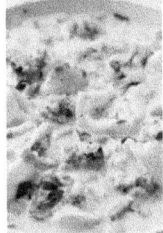

Prep time 10 minutes/ Cook time 30 minutes/ Serves 6

Ingredients
- 1 tablespoon extra-virgin olive oil
- 6 cups beef broth
- 1-pound organic beef sausage, cooked and sliced
- 2 cups sauerkraut
- 2 celery stalks, chopped
- 1 sweet onion, chopped
- 2 teaspoons garlic, minced
- 2 tablespoons butter
- 1 tablespoon hot mustard
- ½ teaspoon caraway seeds
- ½ cup sour cream
- 2 tablespoons fresh parsley, chopped

Directions
1. Grease the inner pot of your Ninja Foodi with olive oil
2. Add broth, sausage, sauerkraut, celery, onion, garlic, butter, mustard, caraway seeds in the pot
3. Lock lid and cook on HIGH pressure for 30 minutes
4. Quick release pressure
5. Remove lid and stir in sour cream
6. Serve with a topping of parsley

Per Serving: Calories: 165, Fat: 4g, Carbohydrates: 14g, Protein: 11g

The Indian Beef Delight

You will absolutely love this recipe! If topped with an avocado, it becomes so sweet and delicious. You can as well drizzle some lime juice and cilantro and they make it better!

Prep time 15 minutes/ Cook time 20 minutes/ Serves 4
Ingredients
- ½ yellow onion, chopped
- 1 tablespoon olive oil
- 2 garlic cloves, minced
- 1 jalapeno pepper, chopped
- 1 cup cherry tomatoes, quartered
- 1 teaspoon fresh lemon juice
- 1-2 pounds grass fed ground beef
- 1-2 pounds fresh collard greens, trimmed and chopped

Spices
- 1 teaspoon cumin, ground
- ½ teaspoon ginger, ground
- 1 teaspoon coriander, ground
- ½ teaspoon fennel seeds, ground
- ½ teaspoon cinnamon, ground
- Salt and pepper to taste
- ½ teaspoon turmeric, ground

Directions
1. Set your Ninja Foodi to sauté mode and add garlic, onions
2. sauté for 3 minutes
3. Add jalapeno pepper, beef and spices
4. Lock lid and cook on Medium-HIGH pressure for 15 minutes
5. Release pressure naturally over 10 minutes, open lid
6. Add tomatoes, collard greens and sauté for 3 minutes
7. Stir in lemon juice, salt and pepper
8. Stir well
9. Once the dish is ready, transfer the dish to your serving bowl and enjoy!

Per Serving: Calories: 409, Fat: 16g, Carbohydrates: 5g, Protein: 56g

Fresh Korean Braised Ribs

This paleo recipe is delicious, simple and soft. It an ideal recipe for summer time and outside cooking.

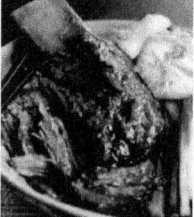

Prep time 10 minutes/ Cook time 45 minutes/ Serves 6
Ingredients
- 1 teaspoon olive oil
- 2 green onions, cut into 1-inch length
- 3 garlic cloves, smashed
- 3 quarter sized ginger slices
- 4 pounds beef short ribs, 3 inches thick, cut into 3 rib portions

- ½ cup water
- ½ cup coconut aminos
- ¼ cup dry white wine
- 2 teaspoons sesame oil
- Mince green onions for serving

Directions
1. Set your Ninja Foodi to "SAUTE" mode and add oil, let it shimmer
2. Add green onions, garlic, ginger, Saute for 1 minute
3. Add short ribs, water, aminos, wine, sesame oil and stir until the ribs are coated well
4. Lock lid and cook on HIGH pressure for 45 minutes
5. Release pressure naturally over 10 minutes
6. Remove short ribs from pot and serve with the cooking liquid

Per Serving: Calories: 423, Fat: 35g, Carbohydrates: 4g, Protein: 22g

The Classical Corned Beef and Cabbage

The cabbage gives the beef a soft and tender taste that will leave you wanting more.

Prep time 15 minutes/ Cook time 90 minutes/ Serves 4

Ingredients
- 3 pounds cabbage, cut into eight wedges
- 1 onion, quartered
- 1 celery stalk, quartered
- 1 corned beef spice packet
- 4 cups water
- 1-pound carrots, peeled and cut to 2 and ½ inch length

Directions
1. Rinse beef thoroughly and add to Ninja Foodi
2. Add onion and celery to the pot
3. Add water and lock lid
4. Cook on HIGH pressure for 90 minutes, quick release pressure
5. Transfer beef to a plate
6. Add carrots, and cabbage to the pot, lock lid again and cook on HIGH pressure for 5 minutes more
7. Quick release pressure
8. Transfer veggies to the plate with corned beef
9. Pass the gravy through a gravy strainer over the beef and serve

Per Serving: Calories: 531, Fat: 45g, Carbohydrates: 9g, Protein: 25g

The Ultimate One-Pot Beef Roast

To give this recipe even a greater taste, spice it up with cloves and Italian seasoning to for a more exotic aroma. This dish goes well with a side of steamed asparagus and you may have a hot sauce on the side to kick things up.

Prep time 10 minutes/ Cook time 40 minutes/ Serves 4
Ingredients
- 2-3 pounds beef, chuck roast
- 4 carrots, chopped
- 3 garlic cloves,
- 2 tablespoons olive oil
- 2 tablespoons Italian seasoning
- 2 stalks celery, chopped
- 1 onion, chopped
- 1 cup beef broth
- 1 cup dry red wine

Directions
- Set your Ninja Foodi to "Saute" mode and add oil, let it heat up
- Add roast beef to the pot and cook each side for 1-2 minute until browned
- Transfer browned beef to plate
- Add celery, carrot to the pot and top with garlic and onion
- Add beef broth and wine to the pot, put roast on top of vegies
- Spread seasoning on top and lock lid, Cook on HIGH pressure for 35 minutes
- Release pressure naturally over 10 minutes

Per Serving: Calories: 299, Fat: 21g, Carbohydrates: 3g, Protein: 14g

Easy to Swallow Beef Ribs

A must do with your Ninja Pot. You don't need a grill to enjoy a barbecue anymore. Right here, is an amazing option to make and guess what, your guests will be all finger licking when they have it.

Prep time 10 minutes/ Cook time 60 minutes/ Serves 6
Ingredients
- 1 tablespoon sesame oil
- 2 garlic cloves, peeled and smashed
- 1 Knob fresh ginger, peeled and finely chopped
- 1 pinch red pepper flakes
- ¼ cup white wine vinegar
- 2/3 cup coconut aminos
- 2/3 cup beef stock
- 4 pounds beef ribs, chopped in half
- 2 tablespoons arrowroot
- 1-2 tablespoons water

Directions
1. Set your Ninja Foodi to Saute mode and add sesame oil, garlic, ginger, red pepper flakes and Saute for 1 minute
2. Deglaze pot with vinegar and mix in coconut aminos and beef stock
3. Add ribs to the pot and coat them well
4. Lock lid and cook on HIGH pressure for 60 minutes
5. Release pressure naturally over 10 minutes
6. Remove the ribs and keep them on the side
7. Take small bowl and mix in arrowroot and water, stir and mix in the liquid into the pot, set the pot to Saute mode and cook until the liquid reaches your desired consistency

8.	Put the ribs under a broiler to brown them slightly (also possible to do this in the Ninja Foodi using the Air Crisping lid)
9.	Serve ribs with the cooking liquid
Per Serving: Calories: 307, Fat: 10g, Carbohydrates: 5g, Protein: 32g

The Gentle Beef and Broccoli Dish

This combo is always on point and it never goes wrong in terms of great taste.

Prep time 10 minutes/ Cook time 20 minutes/ Serves 4
Ingredients
- 3 pounds beef chuck roast, cut into thin strips
- 1 tablespoon olive oil
- 1 yellow onion, peeled and chopped
- ½ cup beef stock
- 1-pound broccoli florets
- 2 teaspoons toasted sesame oil
- 2 tablespoons arrowroot

For Marinade
- 1 cup coconut aminos
- 1 tablespoon sesame oil
- 2 tablespoons fish sauce
- 5 garlic cloves, peeled and minced
- 3 red peppers, dried and crushed
- ½ teaspoon Chinese five spice powder
- Toasted sesame seeds, for serving

Directions
1.	Take a bowl and mix in coconut aminos, fish sauce, 1 tablespoon sesame oil, garlic, five spice powder, crushed red pepper and stir
2.	Add beef strips to the bowl and toss to coat
3.	Keep it on the side for 10 minutes
4.	Set your Ninja Foodi to "Saute" mode and add oil, let it heat up, add onion and stir cook for 4 minutes
5.	Add beef and marinade, stir cook for 2 minutes. Add stock and stir
6.	Lock the pressure lid of Ninja Foodi and cook on HIGH pressure for 5 minutes
7.	Release pressure naturally over 10 minutes
8.	Mix arrowroot with ¼ cup liquid from the pot and gently pour the mixture back to the pot and stir
9.	Place a steamer basket in the pot and add broccoli to the steamer rack, lock lid and cook on HIGH pressure for 3 minutes more, quick release pressure
10.	 Divide the dish between plates and serve with broccoli, toasted sesame seeds and enjoy!
Per Serving: Calories: 433, Fat: 27g, Carbohydrates: 8g, Protein: 20g

The Juicy Beef Chili

This beef chilly is very creamy and juicy. It has many nutrients which are good for the body.

Prep time 10 minutes/ Cook time 40 minutes/ Serves 4

Ingredients
- 1 and ½ pounds ground beef
- 1 sweet onion, peeled and chopped
- Salt and pepper to taste
- 28 ounces canned tomatoes, diced
- 17 ounces beef stock
- 6 garlic clove, peeled and chopped
- 7 jalapeno peppers, diced
- 2 tablespoons olive oil
- 4 carrots, peeled and chopped
- 3 tablespoons chili powder
- 1 bay leaf
- 1 teaspoon chili powder

Directions
1. Set your Ninja Foodi to "Saute" mode and add half of oil, let it heat up
2. Add beef and stir brown for 8 minutes, transfer to a bowl
3. Add remaining oil to the pot and let it heat up, add carrots, onion, jalapenos, garlic and stir Saute for 4 minutes
4. Add tomatoes and stir
5. Add bay leaf, stock, chili powder, chili powder, salt, pepper and beef, stir and lock lid
6. Cook on HIGH pressure for 25 minutes
7. Release pressure naturally over 10 minutes
8. Stir the chili and serve

Per Serving: Calories: 448, Fat: 22g, Carbohydrates: 7g, Protein: 15g

Generous Ground Beef Stew

Trust me, the aromas and tastes of this recipe are good and you will be glad that you tried it.

Prep time 5 minutes/ Cook time 5 minutes/ Serves 4

Ingredients
- 1 tablespoon olive oil
- 1 and ½ pounds lean ground beef
- 1 large yellow onion, chopped
- 1 teaspoon ground cinnamon
- 1 teaspoon ground cumin
- ½ teaspoon dried sage
- ½ teaspoon dried oregano
- ½ teaspoon salt
- ½ teaspoon pepper

- 2 tablespoons almond meal
- 2 and ½ cups beef broth
- 2 teaspoons stevia

Directions
1. Set your Ninja Foodi to Saute mode and add oil, let it heat up
2. Add ground beef and stir for about 5 minutes until browned
3. Add onion, and cook for 3 minutes more
4. Stir in cinnamon, cumin, sage, oregano, salt, pepper and cook for 1 minute
5. Stir in almond meal and cook for 1 minute more
6. Stir in broth
7. Lock lid and cook on HIGH pressure for 5 minutes, release pressure naturally over 10 minutes
8. Stir well until loosely covered, serve and enjoy!

Per Serving: Calories: 480, Fat: 23g, Carbohydrates: 12g, Protein: 20g

Spiced Beef Shapes

The beef shapes are many people's favorite, especially among the kids. They are a good deal on a birthday.

Prep time 30 minutes/ Cook time 15 minutes/ Serves 12

Ingredients:
- 1 ½ lb ground beef
- ½ cup minced onion
- 2 tbsp chopped mint leaves
- 3 garlic cloves, minced
- 2 tsp paprika
- 2 tsp coriander seeds
- ½ tsp cayenne pepper
- 1 tsp salt
- 1 tbsp chopped parsley
- 2 tsp cumin
- ½ tsp ground ginger

Directions:
1. Soak 24 skewers in water, until ready to use.
2. Preheat the Ninja Air fryer to 330 degrees F.
3. Combine all ingredients in a large bowl.
4. Make sure to mix well with your hands until the herbs and spices are evenly distributed, and the mixture is well incorporated.
5. Shape the beef mixture into 12 shapes around 2 skewers.
6. Cook for 12 - 15 minutes on Air Fry mode, or until preferred doneness.
7. Serve with tzatziki sauce and enjoy.

Per serving: Calories 304, Carbohydrates 13g, Fat 16g, Protein 21g

Thai Roasted Beef

This hearty and hot recipe is good for dinner stew. This is a popular Thai recipe and it has become popular in many parts of the world.

Prep time 4 hours/ Cook time 20 minutes/ Serves 2
Ingredients:
- 1 lb. ground beef
- ½ tsp salt
- 2 tbsp soy sauce
- ½ tsp pepper
- Thumb-sized piece of ginger, chopped
- 3 chilies, deseeded and chopped
- 4 garlic cloves, chopped
- 1 tsp brown sugar
- Juice of 1 lime
- 2 tbsp mirin
- 2 tbsp coriander, chopped
- 2 tbsp basil, chopped
- 2 tbsp oil
- 2 tbsp fish sauce

Directions:
1. Place all ingredients, except beef, salt, and pepper, in a blender; pulse until smooth.
2. Season the beef with salt and pepper. Place the meat and Thai mixture in a zipper bag. Shake well to combine and let marinate in the fridge for about 4 hours.
3. Preheat the Ninja Air fryer to 350 degrees.
4. Place the beef in the air fryer basket and cook for about 12 minutes, or more if you like it well done, on Air Fry mode. Let sit for 5 minutes before serving.

Per serving: Calories 678, Carbohydrates 21g, Fat 39g, Protein 64g

Peppercorn Meatloaf

This recipe is so tasty and colorful at the same time. It takes less than an hour to get ready! It is also spicy and full of sweet flavors from its ingredients

Prep time 10 minutes/ Cook time 35 minutes/ Serves 8
Ingredients:
- 4 lb. ground beef
- 1 tbsp basil
- 1 tbsp oregano
- 1 tbsp parsley
- 1 onion, diced
- 1 tbsp Worcestershire sauce
- 3 tbsp ketchup
- ½ tsp salt
- 1 tsp ground peppercorns

- 10 whole peppercorns, for garnishing
- 1 cup breadcrumbs

Directions:
1. Preheat the Ninja Air fryer to 350 degrees F. Place the beef in a large bowl.
2. Add all of the ingredients except the whole peppercorns and the breadcrumbs.
3. Mix with your hand until well combined. Stir in the breadcrumbs.
4. Put the meatloaf on a lined baking dish.
5. Insert in the air fryer and cook for 25 minutes on Air Fry mode.
6. Garnish the meatloaf with the whole peppercorns and let cool slightly before serving.

Per serving: Calories 613, Carbohydrates 18g, Fat 27g, Protein 41g

Beef Congee with Kale

This delicious recipe makes you enjoy and appreciate beef's greatness. The other ingredients will make you love the recipe and want to have them more often! The combination with the kale makes this recipe so amazing for every meat lover.

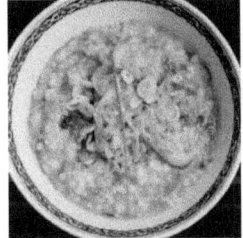

Prep time 10 minutes/ Cook time 30 minutes/ Serves 6

Ingredients:
- 2 pounds ground beef
- 1-inch piece ginger, minced
- 2 cloves garlic, minced
- 6 cups beef stock
- 1 cup kale, roughly chopped
- 1 cup jasmine rice, uncooked, rinsed and drained
- 1 cups water
- Ground black pepper and salt to taste
- Fresh cilantro, chopped

Directions:
1. Take Ninja Foodi multi-cooker, arrange it over a cooking platform, and open the top lid.
2. In the pot, add the garlic, rice, and ginger.
3. Add the stock and water. Stir the mixture and add the beef.
4. Seal the multi-cooker by locking it with the pressure lid; ensure to keep the pressure release valve locked/sealed.
5. Select "pressure" mode and select the "hi" pressure level. Then, set timer to 30 minutes and press "stop/start"; it will start the cooking process by building up inside pressure.
6. When the timer goes off, quick release pressure by adjusting the pressure valve to the vent. After pressure gets released, open the pressure lid.
7. Stir in the kale. Add pepper and salt for seasoning. Serve warm with some cilantro on top and enjoy!

Per Serving: Calories: 328, Fat: 15g, Carbs: 12g, Protein: 37g

Beef Pasta Mania

Here is another easy to make recipe, it should take you less than 15 minutes to complete your Beef Pasta.

Prep time 5 minutes/ Cook time 10 minutes/ Serves 4
Ingredients:
- 1 tablespoon extra-virgin olive oil
- 2 pounds beef, ground
- 1 cup water
- 1 cup dry red wine
- 2 jars marinara sauce
- 1 pack ziti pasta
- ½ teaspoon sea salt
- ½ teaspoon garlic powder
- 1 cup shredded mozzarella cheese
- 1 cup ricotta cheese
- ½ cup chopped fresh parsley

Directions:
1. Take Ninja Foodi multi-cooker, arrange it over a cooking platform, and open the top lid.
2. In the pot, add the oil; Select "sear/sauté" mode and select "md: hi" pressure level.
3. Press "stop/start." After about 4-5 minutes, the oil will start simmering.
4. Add the beef and stir cook for about 6-8 minutes to brown evenly.
5. Add the marinara sauce, water, wine, and pasts; stir and season with the garlic powder and salt.
6. Seal the multi-cooker by locking it with the pressure lid; ensure to keep the pressure release valve locked/sealed.
7. Select "pressure" mode and select the "lo" pressure level. Then, set timer to 2 minutes and press "stop/start"; it will start the cooking process by building up inside pressure.
8. When the timer goes off, naturally release inside pressure for about 8-10 minutes. Then, quick-release pressure by adjusting the pressure valve to the vent.
9. Stir in the ricotta and mozzarella cheese.
10. Seal the multi-cooker by locking it with the crisping lid; ensure to keep the pressure release valve locked/sealed.
11. Select "broil" mode and select the "HI" pressure level. Then, set timer to 3 minutes and press "stop/start"; it will start the cooking process by building up inside pressure.
12. When the timer goes off, quick release pressure by adjusting the pressure valve to the vent.
13. After pressure gets released, open the pressure lid.
14. Serve warm with some parsley on top and enjoy!

Per Serving: Calories: 741, Fat: 31.5g, Carbohydrates: 52.5g, Protein: 57g

Beef Meatballs in Honey-Orange Sauce

Having a Ninja Pot without making meatballs is not permissible. You need to make this once and many times for yourself and your guests.

Prep time 15 minutes/ Cook time 28 minutes/ Serves: 4
Ingredients:

- 1 ½ lb. ground beef
- 2 large eggs, lightly beaten
- ¼ cup evaporated milk
- 1/3 cup orange marmalade
- 2 tbsp freshly chopped scallions for garnishing
- ½ cup panko breadcrumbs
- 1 tsp garlic powder
- 1 tsp cumin powder
- 2 shallots, finely chopped
- Salt and freshly ground black pepper to taste
- 1 tsp + 1/3 cup honey
- 2 tbsp butter, melted
- 2 tbsp cornstarch
- 2 tbsp soy sauce
- 2 tbsp hot sauce
- 1/3 cup firmly packed brown sugar
- 1 tbsp Worcestershire sauce
- ½ cup chicken broth

Directions

1. Fix the Cook & Crisp basket into the inner pot. Close the Air Crisping Lid. Select Air Crisp, set the temperature to 400°F, and the time to 5 minutes. Choose Start/Stop to preheat the lid.
2. Meanwhile, in a large bowl, combine the beef, breadcrumbs, eggs, milk, garlic powder, cumin powder, shallots, salt, black pepper, and 1 tsp of honey until well mixed. Mold 1 ½-inch meatballs from the mixture.
3. When the lid is done preheating, open and arrange the meatballs in the basket; grease with cooking spray.
4. Close the Air Crisping Lid. Select Air Crisp, set the temperature to 400°F, and the time to 15 minutes. Choose Start/Stop to start frying the meatballs.
5. Halfway through the cook, open the lid and turn the meatballs. Continue cooking until crispy, brown, and cooked within. Open the lid and remove the meatballs onto a serving plate. Set aside for serving. Remove the basket from the pot.
6. Select Sear/Sauté on the pot and set to Medium High. Choose Start/Stop to preheat the pot for 5 minutes.
7. Melt the butter in the inner pot and mix in the orange marmalade, corn starch, soy sauce, hot sauce, brown sugar, honey, Worcestershire sauce, and chicken broth until well mixed.
8. Allow simmering for 5 to 8 minutes or until the sauce becomes syrupy and slightly thickened.
9. Pour the meatballs into the sauce and coat well with the sauce.
10. Dish the food, garnish with the scallions, and serve warm.

Per Serving: Calories 912, Fats 37.7g, Carbs 100.1g, Protein 46.57g

Spicy Beef Pitas

This recipe is so spiced up and it is full of flavors. You will enjoy every bit of it.

Prep time 15 minutes/ Cook time 39 minutes/ Serves: 4

Ingredients:
- 1 lb. beef stew meat, cut into strips
- 1 medium tomato, chopped
- 1 large cucumber, deseeded and chopped
- 4 whole pita breads, warmed

- 1 cup Greek yogurt
- 1 tbsp olive oil
- Salt and freshly ground black pepper to taste
- 1 small white onion, chopped
- 3 garlic cloves, minced
- 1 tsp dried oregano
- 2 tsp hot sauce
- ¼ cup beef broth
- 1 tsp dried dill

Directions
1. Select Sear/Sauté and set to High. Choose Start/Stop to preheat the pot for 5 minutes.
2. Heat the olive oil in the inner pot, season the meat with salt, black pepper, and sear in the oil until brown, 5 minutes. Transfer the meat to a plate and set aside.
3. Add the onion to the oil and cook until softened, 3 minutes. Stir in the garlic, oregano and cook until fragrant, 30 seconds. Stir in the hot sauce and beef broth.
4. Cover with the Pressure Lid and lock the vent to Seal. Select Pressure and set to High. Set the time to 20 minutes. Choose Start/Stop to begin cooking.
5. When the timer is done, perform a natural pressure release for 10 minutes, then a quick pressure release, and carefully open the lid.
6. Stir in the tomato, cucumber, and spoon the mixture into the pita breads.
7. In a medium bowl, mix the dill and yogurt, and top on the pita filling.
8. Serve immediately.

Per Serving: Calories 312, Carbs 24.28g, Fats 11g, Protein 31.18g

CHAPTER 6: PORK 30 RECIPES

Broccoli Pork with Rice

It is amazing how this pork cooks in very little time than expected and this should be the case when cooking meat to not kill the nutrients in the food.

Prep time 5 minutes/ Cook time 14 minutes/ Serves 4

Ingredients:
- 1 head broccoli, cut into florets
- 1 tablespoon extra-virgin olive oil
- ¼ teaspoon black pepper
- ¼ teaspoon sea salt
- 1 cup long-grain white rice
- 1 cup water
- 1 trimmed pork tenderloin, cut into 1-inch pieces
- 1 cup teriyaki sauce
- Sesame seeds to garnish

Directions:
1. In a mixing bowl, combine the broccoli with the olive oil. Season with the ground black pepper and salt.
2. In another bowl, combine the sauce and pork until evenly coated.
3. Take Ninja Foodi multi-cooker, arrange it over a cooking platform, and open the top lid.
4. In the pot, add the water and rice.
5. Seal the multi-cooker by locking it with the pressure lid; ensure to keep the pressure release valve locked/sealed.
6. Select "pressure" mode and select the "HI" pressure level. Then, set timer to 2 minutes and press "stop/start"; it will start the cooking process by building up inside pressure.
7. When the timer goes off, quick release pressure by adjusting the pressure valve to the vent. After pressure gets released, open the pressure lid.
8. Over the rice, arrange the reversible rack and place the pork and broccoli over the rack.
9. Seal the multi-cooker by locking it with the crisping lid; ensure to keep the pressure release valve locked/sealed.
10. Select "broil" mode and select the "HI" pressure level. Then, set timer to 12 minutes and press "stop/start"; it will start the cooking process by building up inside pressure.
11. When the timer goes off, quick release pressure by adjusting the pressure valve to the vent.
12. After pressure gets released, open the pressure lid.
13. Serve the pork mixture warm with the cooked rice and some sesame seeds on top.

Per Serving: Calories: 453, Fats 9.5g, Carbs: 52g, Protein: 39g

Tangy Pork Carnitas

This is a very delicious pork carnitas that takes less than an hour to make. It is amazing with the Ninja Foodi, and Air Crisp function makes it very crispy. This recipe starts by first pressure cooking the pork, and then air crisping them, all in one device.

Prep time 10 minutes/ Cook time 25 minutes/ Serves 6

Ingredients:
- 2 pounds pork shoulder, bone-in
- 2 tablespoons butter, melted
- 2 oranges, juiced
- Ground black pepper and salt to taste
- 1 teaspoon garlic powder
- 5-6 warmed carnitas

Directions:
1. Season the pork with salt, garlic powder, and black pepper.
2. Take Ninja Foodi multi-cooker, arrange it over a cooking platform, and open the top lid.
3. In the pot, add the butter; Select "sear/sauté" mode and select "md: hi" pressure level.
4. Press "stop/start." After about 4-5 minutes, the butter will start simmering.
5. Add the meat and stir cook for about 2-3 minutes to brown evenly. Stir in orange juice.
6. Seal the multi-cooker by locking it with the pressure lid; ensure to keep the pressure release valve locked/sealed.
7. Select "pressure" mode and select the "HI" pressure level. Then, set timer to 15 minutes and press "stop/start"; it will start the cooking process by building up inside pressure.
8. When the timer goes off, naturally release inside pressure for about 8-10 minutes. Then, quick-release pressure by adjusting the pressure valve to the vent.
9. Select "broil" mode and select the "HI" pressure level. Then, set timer to 15 minutes and press "stop/start"; it will start the cooking process by building up inside pressure.
10. When the timer goes off, quick release pressure by adjusting the pressure valve to the vent.
11. After pressure gets released, open the pressure lid.
12. Shred the meat and remove the bones. Add the mixture over the carnitas; fold and serve warm.

Per Serving: Calories: 486, Fat: 32g, Carbs: 9g, Protein: 34g

Bourbon Pork Chops

Pork chops rarely disappoint when it comes to delicious taste and nutrition and this recipe is no exception! It can be topped with apples, onions, green veggies or sweet potatoes.

Prep time 5 minutes/ Cook time 20 minutes/ Serves 4

Ingredients:
- 4 boneless pork chops
- Sea salt and ground black pepper
- ¼ cup apple cider vinegar
- ¼ cup soy sauce
- 3 tablespoons Worcestershire sauce
- 2 cups ketchup
- ¾ cup bourbon

- 1 cup packed brown sugar
- ½ tablespoon dry mustard powder

Directions:
1. Take Ninja Foodi Grill, arrange it over your kitchen platform, and open the top lid. Arrange the grill grate and close the top lid.
2. Press "grill" and select the "med" grill function. Adjust the timer to 15 minutes and then press "start/stop." Ninja Foodi will start preheating.
3. Ninja Foodi is preheated and ready to cook when it starts to beep. After you hear a beep, open the top lid.
4. Arrange the pork chops over the grill grate.
5. Close the top lid and cook for 8 minutes. Now open the top lid, flip the pork chops.
6. Close the top lid and cook for 8 more minutes. Check the pork chops for doneness, cook for 2 more minutes if required.
7. In a saucepan, heat the soy sauce, sugar, ketchup, bourbon, vinegar, Worcestershire sauce, and mustard powder; stir-cook until boils.
8. Reduce heat and simmer for 20 minutes to thicken the sauce.
9. Season the pork chops with salt and black pepper. Serve warm with the prepared sauce.

Per Serving: Calories: 346, Fat: 13.5g, Carbohydrates: 27g, Protein: 27g

Classic Pork Meal with Green Bean

A lot of people love to have their meat juicy and tender on the inside, and very crispy on the outside. This Pork recipe will do just that, not only this, it is very crunchy and delicious.

Prep time 5 minutes/ Cook time 25 minutes/ Serves 4

Ingredients:
- 2 pounds pork stew meat, cut into small cubes
- 1 tablespoon avocado oil
- 1-pound green beans, trimmed and halved
- 2 minced garlic cloves
- 1 tablespoon basil, chopped
- 1 teaspoon chili powder
- ¾ cup veggie stock
- A pinch of black pepper and salt

Directions:
1. Take Ninja Foodi multi-cooker, arrange it over a cooking platform, and open the top lid.
2. In the pot, add the oil; Select "sear/sauté" mode and select "md: hi" pressure level.
3. Press "stop/start." After about 4-5 minutes, the oil will start simmering.
4. Add the meat, garlic, and stir-cook for about 4-5 minutes to brown evenly.
5. Add the remaining ingredients; stir well.
6. Seal the multi-cooker by locking it with the pressure lid; ensure to keep the pressure release valve locked/sealed.
7. Select "pressure" mode and select the "HI" pressure level. Then, set timer to 20 minutes and press "stop/start"; it will start the cooking process by building up inside pressure.
8. When the timer goes off, naturally release inside pressure for about 8-10 minutes. Then, quick-release pressure by adjusting the pressure valve to the vent.
9. After pressure gets released, open the pressure lid.
10. Serve warm.

Per Serving: Calories: 403, Fat: 15.5g, Carbs: 18g, Protein: 53.5g

Southern-Style Lettuce Wraps

They are so simple and delicious. And they are very interchangeable. You can make so many versions by swapping out the proteins and garnish.

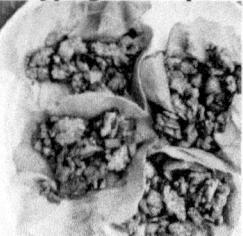

They are so simple and delicious. And they are very interchangeable. You can make so many versions by swapping out the proteins and garnish. Whether you want to go Mexican and incorporate taco toppings or even just traditional with Asian flavors, the possibilities are endless.

Prep time 10 minutes/ Cook time 30 minutes/ Serves 6

Ingredients
- 3 pounds boneless pork shoulder, cut into 1- to 2-inch cubes
- 2 cups light beer
- 1 cup brown sugar
- 1 teaspoon chipotle chiles in adobo sauce
- 1 cup barbecue sauce
- 1 head iceberg lettuce, quartered and leaves separated
- 1 cup roasted peanuts, chopped or ground
- Cilantro leaves

Directions
1. Place the pork, beer, brown sugar, chipotle, and barbecue sauce in the pot. Assemble pressure lid, making sure the pressure release valve is in the seal position.
2. Select pressure and set to HI. Set the timer to 30 minutes. Select start/stop to begin.
3. When pressure cooking is complete, quick release the pressure by turning the pressure release valve to the vent position. Carefully remove lid when unit has finished releasing pressure.
4. Using a silicone-tipped utensil, shred the pork in the pot. Stir to mix the meat in with the sauce.
5. Place a small amount of pork in a piece of lettuce. Top with peanuts and cilantro to serve.

Per serving: Calories: 811, Fats 58g, Carbs: 22g, Protein: 45g

Orecchiette and Pork Ragu

Don't let the recipe title intimidate you. It's just a fancy name for pasta and meat sauce. While a traditional ragu is braised on the stovetop for hours, this version comes together in under 30 minutes thanks to the NinjaFood Pressure Cooker.

Prep time 10 minutes/ Cook time 25 minutes/ Serves 6

Ingredients:
- 3 tablespoons extra-virgin olive oil, divided
- 1-pound pork shoulder, cut into large pieces
- 1 small onion, diced
- 1 carrot, diced
- 1 celery stalk, diced
- 1 garlic clove, minced
- 1 can crushed tomatoes

- 1 can tomato purée
- 1 cup red wine
- 2 cups beef stock
- 1 box orecchiette pasta
- 1 teaspoon sea salt
- 1 teaspoon Italian seasoning
- 1 bunch Tuscan kale, ribs and stems removed, torn
- ¼ cup unsalted butter, cubed
- ½ cup grated Parmesan cheese

Directions
1. Select sear/sauté and set to HI. Select start/stop to begin. Let preheat for 5 minutes.
2. Place 2 tablespoons of oil in the pot. Once hot, add the pork pieces and sear on all sides, turning until brown, about 10 minutes in total. Transfer the pork to a large plate and set aside.
3. Add onion, carrot, and celery and cook for about 5 minutes. Add the garlic and cook for 1 minute.
4. Add the crushed tomatoes, tomato purée, red wine, beef stock, pasta, salt, and Italian seasoning. Place the pork back in the pot. Assemble pressure lid, making sure the pressure release valve is in the SEAL position.
5. Select pressure and set to LO. Set time to 0 minutes. Select start/stop to begin.
6. When pressure cooking is complete, allow pressure to naturally release for 10 minutes. After 10 minutes, quick release remaining pressure by moving the pressure release valve to the vent position. Carefully remove lid when unit has finished releasing pressure.
7. Pull the pork pieces apart using two forks. Add the remaining 1 tablespoon of olive oil, kale, butter, and Parmesan cheese and stir until the butter melts and the kale is wilted. Serve.

Per serving: Calories: 556, Fat: 21g, Carbs: 59g, Protein: 30g

Mustard Dredged Pork Chops

Prep time 10 minutes/ Cook time 30 minutes/ Serves 4
Ingredients
- 2 tablespoons butter
- 2 tablespoons Dijon mustard
- 4 pork chops
- Salt and pepper to taste
- 1 tablespoon fresh rosemary, coarsely chopped

Directions
1. Take a bowl and add pork chops, cover with Dijon mustard and carefully sprinkle rosemary, salt and pepper
2. Let it marinate for 2 hours
3. Add butter and marinated pork chops to your Ninja Foodi pot
4. Lock lid and cook on Low-Medium Pressure for 30 minutes
5. Release pressure naturally over 10 minutes
6. Take the dish out, serve and enjoy!

Per Serving: Calories: 315, Fat: 26g, Carbs:1g Protein: 18g

Authentic Beginner Friendly Pork Belly

Really simple recipe, but filled with a lot of good nutrients. It cooks in no time, so you needn't worry when you get trapped in hunger. Put everything together in the pot, hit start, and get your plate ready.

Prep time 10 minutes/ Cook time 10 minutes/ Serves 4
Ingredients
- 1-pound pork belly
- ½-1 cup white wine vinegar
- 1 garlic clove
- 1 tablespoon olive oil
- Salt and pepper to taste

Directions
1. Set your Ninja Foodi to "sauté" mode and add oil, let it heat up
2. Add pork and sear for 2-3 minutes until both sides are golden and crispy
3. Add vinegar until about a quarter inch, season with salt, pepper and garlic
4. Add garlic clove and Saute until the liquid comes to a boil
5. Lock lid and cook on high pressure for 40 minutes
6. Once done, quick release pressure
7. Slice the meat and serve with the sauce
8. Enjoy!

Per Serving: Calories: 331, Fat: 21g, Carbs: 2g, Protein: 19g

Deliciously Spicy Pork Salad Bowl

The question is, have you ever eaten anything made from pork and chicken stock and the taste is not out of this world? The same is for this recipe; it has gotten very popular because of how great it tastes and how easy to cook it is.

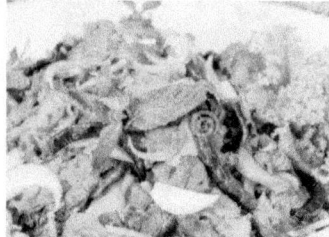

Prep time 10 minutes/ Cook time 90 minutes/ Serves 6
Ingredients
- 4 pounds pork shoulder
- Butter as needed
- 2 teaspoons salt
- 2 cups chicken stock
- 1 teaspoon smoked paprika powder
- 1 teaspoon garlic powder
- 1 teaspoon black pepper
- 1 pinch dried oregano leaves
- 4 tablespoons coconut oil
- 6 garlic cloves

Directions
1. Remove rind from pork and cut meat from bone, slice into large chunks
2. Trim fat off met
3. Set your Foodi to Saute mode and add oil, let it heat up

4. Once the oil is hot, layer chunks of meat in the bottom of the pot and Saute for around 30 minutes until browned
5. While the meat is being browned, peel garlic cloves and cut into small chunks
6. Once the meat is browned, transfer it to a large sized bowl
7. Add a few tablespoons of chicken stock to the pot an deglaze it, scraping off browned bits
8. Transfer browned bits to the bowl with meat chunks
9. Repeat if any more meat is left
10. Once done, add garlic, oregano leaves, smoked paprika, Garlic powder, pepper and salt to the meat owl and mix it up
11. Add all chicken stock to pot and bring to a simmer over Saute mode
12. Once done, return seasoned meat to the pot and lock lid, cook on high pressure for 45 minutes. Release pressure naturally over 10 minutes
13. Open lid and shred the meat using fork, transfer shredded meat to a bowl and pour cooking liquid through a mesh to separate fat into the bowl with shredded meat
14. Serve with lime and enjoy!

Per Serving: Calories: 307, Fat: 23g, Carbs: 8g, Protein: 15g

Special "Swiss" Pork chops

The good part is how good the Pork chops look after the cooking complete; the awesomeness of the ribs is absolutely mesmerizing.

Prep time 5 minutes/ Cook time 18 minutes/ Serves 4

Ingredients
- ½ cup Swiss cheese, shredded
- 4 pork chops, bone-in
- 6 bacon strips, cut in half
- Salt and pepper to taste
- 1 tablespoon butter

Directions
1. Season pork chops with salt and pepper
2. Set your Foodi to sauté mode and add butter, let the butter heat up
3. Add pork chops and sauté for 3 minutes on each side
4. Add bacon strips and Swiss cheese
5. Lock lid and cook on Medium-low pressure for 15 minutes
6. Release pressure naturally over 10 minutes
7. Transfer steaks to serving platter, serve and enjoy!

Per Serving: Calories: 483, Fat: 40g, Carbohydrates:0.7g, Protein: 27g

Perfect Sichuan Pork Soup

It is a dish that is very easy to make, and it takes very little time to prepare. It takes about 10 minutes of preparation time, and about 20 minutes of cooking time.

Prep time 10 minutes/ Cook time 20 minutes/ Serves 6
Ingredients
- 2 tablespoons olive oil
- 1 tablespoon garlic, minced
- 1 tablespoon fresh ginger, minced
- 2 tablespoons coconut aminos
- 2 tablespoons black vinegar
- 1-2 teaspoons stevia
- 1-2 teaspoons salt
- ½ onion, sliced
- 1-pound pork shoulder, cut into 2-inch chunks
- 2 pepper corns, crushed
- 3 cups water
- 3-4 cups bok choy, chopped
- ¼ cup fresh cilantro, chopped

Directions
1. Pre-heat your Ninja Foodi by setting it to Saute mode on HIGH settings
2. Once the inner pot it hot enough, add oil and let heat until shimmering
3. Add garlic and ginger and Saute for 1-2 minutes
4. Add coconut aminos, vinegar, sweetener, pepper corn, salt, onion, pork, water and stir
5. Lock lid and cook on high pressure for 20 minutes
6. Release pressure naturally over 10 minutes
7. Open lid and add bok choy, close lid and let it cook in the remaining heat for 10 minutes
8. Ladle soup into serving bowl and serve with topping of cilantro
9. Enjoy!

Per Serving: Calories: 256, Fat: 20g, Carbs: 5g, Protein: 14g

Healthy Cranberry BBQ Pork

This is must do with your Ninja Pot. You don't need a grill to enjoy a barbecue anymore. The Ninja Foodi does the BBQ for you and your guests will be all finger licking when eating it.

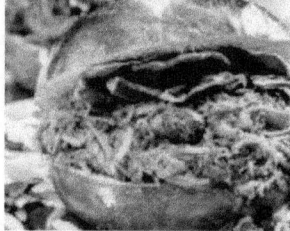

Prep time 10 minutes/ Cook time 45 minutes/ Serves 4
Ingredients
- 3-4 pounds pork shoulder, boneless, fat trimmed
- 3 tablespoons liquid smoke
- 2 tablespoons tomato paste
- 2 cups fresh cranberries
- ¼ cup hot sauce
- 1/3 cup blackstrap molasses
- ½ cup water
- ½ cup apple cider vinegar
- 1 teaspoon salt
- 1 tablespoons adobo sauce
- 1 cup tomato puree
- 1 chipotle pepper in adobo sauce, diced

Directions
1. Cut pork against halves/thirds and keep it on the side
2. Set your Ninja Foodi to "sauté" mode and let it heat up

3. Add cranberries and water to the pot
4. Let them simmer for 4-5 minutes until cranberries start to pop, add rest of the sauce ingredients and simmer for 5 minutes more
5. Add pork to the pot and lock lid
6. Cook on high pressure for 40 minutes
7. Quick release pressure
8. Use fork to shred the pork and serve on your favorite greens

Per Serving: Calories: 250, Fat: 17g, Carbs: 5g, Protein: 15g

Decisive Kalua Pork

A bit of protein, a bit of good fat, and a bit of vitamins is what you have right here in this recipe. You can make some more steamed veggies to enjoy the sauce with or have it with a side of steamed green beans.

Prep time 10 minutes/ Cook time 90 minutes/ Serves 4

Ingredients
- 4 pounds pork shoulder, cut into half
- ½ cup water
- 2 tablespoons olive oil
- Salt and pepper to taste
- 1 tablespoon liquid smoke
- Steamer green beans for serving

Directions
1. Set your Ninja Foodi to "sauté" mode and add oil, let it heat up
2. Add pork, salt and pepper, brown each side for 3 minutes until both sides are slightly browned
3. Transfer them to a plate
4. Add water, liquid smoke to the pot and return the meat, stir
5. Lock lid and cook on high pressure for 90 minutes, release pressure naturally over 10 minutes
6. Transfer meat to cutting board and shred using 2 forks, divide between serving plates and serve with the cooking liquid on top, add green beans on the side if you prefer
7. Enjoy!

Per Serving: Calories: 357, Fat: 28g, Carbs: 2g, Protein: 20g

Easy-Going Kid Friendly Pork Chops

With less than ingredients giving you creamy goodness, what else can you wish for? Put all the ingredients in the Ninja Pot, hit Start, and rush to get a quick shower. On return, the dish will be near done to fill up your hungry tummy.

Prep time 15 minutes/ Cook time 10 minutes/ Serves 4

Ingredients
- 3-4 pork chops -12 to ¾ inch thick each
- 1 egg, beaten
- 1-2 cups Almond flour as needed

- Salt and pepper to taste
- 1-2 cups almond meal
- ½ cup onions, chopped
- 2-4 garlic cloves, squashed and chopped
- 1 tablespoons butter
- 1-2 tablespoons coconut oil

Directions
1. Set your Ninja Foodi to "Saute" mode and add butter, let it heat up
2. Dredge the pork chops in beaten egg, then in flour and finally in almond meal
3. Add them to the pot and brown all sides
4. Add onions and cook for a minute
5. Add garlic and cook for 1 minute more
6. Transfer the browned meat, onion and garlic to a plate, make sure to keep the drippings in the pot
7. Add 2-3 tablespoons of water and place and place a steamer rack in your pot
8. Add browned pork chops on the steamer and lock lid
9. Cook on high Pressure for 5 minutes, once done, let the pressure release naturally over 10 minutes
10. Remove from pot and serve
11. Enjoy!

Per Serving: Calories: 446, Fat: 25g Carbs: 6g Protein: 21g

Amazing Mexican Pulled Pork Lettuce

Even though this recipe is very easy to make, it takes a long of time, a very long time. The good thing is that with your Foodi, it should be faster, and the second thing is that it does not really require you to do much.

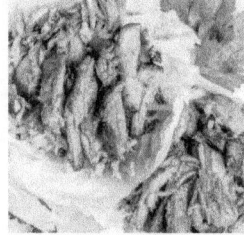

Prep time 10 minutes/ Cook time 60 minutes/ Serves 4

Ingredients
- 4 pounds pork roast
- 1 head butter lettuce, washed and dried
- 2 carrots, grated
- 2 tablespoons olive oil
- 2 lime wedges
- 1 onion, chopped
- 1 tablespoon salt
- 2-3 cups water
- 1 tablespoon unsweetened cocoa powder
- 2 teaspoons oregano
- 1 teaspoon red pepper flakes
- 1 teaspoon garlic powder
- 1 teaspoon white pepper
- 1 teaspoon cumin
- 1/8 teaspoon cayenne
- 1/8 teaspoon coriander

Directions
1. Marinate pork overnight by transferring the meat to a bowl and mixing in all of the spices
2. Set your Ninja Foodi to "saute" mode and add roast, let it brown
3. Add 2-3 cups water to fully submerge the roast
4. Lock lid and cook on HIGH pressure for 55 minutes
5. Release pressure naturally over 10 minutes

6. Set your pot to "saute" mode again and take out the meat, shred the meat and keep it on the side
7. Reduce the liquid by half and strain/skim any excess fat
8. Mix pork with cooking liquid and serve with lettuce, grated carrots, squire of lime and any other topping you desire
9. Enjoy!

Per Serving: Calories: 245 Fat: 18g Carbs:4g Protein: 13g

Bacon Pork Chops

It is probably one of the easiest recipes out there, because it is just ideal for a lazy day or when you do not feel like doing much in the kitchen.

Prep time 10 minutes/ Cook time 18 minutes/ Serves 4

Ingredients:
- ½ cup Swiss cheese, shredded
- 4 pork chops, bone-in
- 6 bacon strips, cut in half
- Salt and black pepper, to taste
- 1 tablespoon butter

Directions
1. Season pork chops with pepper and salt.
2. Turn on Ninja Foodi and select sauté.
3. Add butter, pork chops and sauté for 3 minutes on each side.
4. Add cheese and bacon strips.
5. Close the lid and select "pressure."
6. Set timer to 15 minutes on "Medium Low."
7. Transfer steaks in serving plate and serve.

Per Serving: Calories 483, Fat 40 g, Carbs 0.7 g, Protein 27.7 g

Jamaican Jerk Pork Roast

The good thing about pork is that it can be used for multiple purposes. This recipe will easily be one your favorites, and the fact that you do not have to transfer it elsewhere after cooking means that making it with the Ninja Foodi will make it super easy for you.

Prep time 15 minutes/ Cook time 23 minutes/ Serves 3

Ingredients:
- 1 tablespoon butter
- 1/8 cup beef broth
- 1-pound pork shoulder
- 1/8 cup Jamaican jerk spice blend

Directions
1. Season pork with Jamaican jerk spice.
2. Turn on the Ninja Foodi and select sauté.

3. Add butter, broth, seasoned pork and sauté for 3 minutes
4. Close the lid and press "pressure."
5. Set the timer for 20 minutes on low and release pressure naturally.
6. Serve and enjoy.

Per Serving: Calories 477, Fat 36.2 g Carbs 0 g, Protein 35.4 g

Pork Carnitas

Unlike many other recipes that I have explained, the Crispy Pork Carnitas uses both the pressure cooking and the air crisping function of the Foodi. If the appliance is new and you are just still trying to understand how it works both ways, then this recipe is the perfect way to put both the pressure cooking and air crisping function to test.

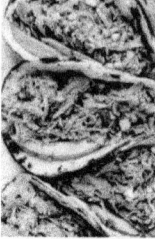

Prep time 15 minutes/ Cook time 26 minutes/ Serves 6

Ingredients:
- 2 tablespoons butter
- 2 oranges, juiced
- 2 pounds pork shoulder, bone-in
- Salt and black pepper, to taste
- 1 teaspoon garlic powder

Directions
1. Season pork with salt and black pepper.
2. Turn on the Ninja Foodi and select sauté.
3. Add butter, garlic powder and sauté for 1 minute.
4. Add seasoned pork and sauté for 3 minutes.
5. Stir in orange juice and close the lid.
6. Select "pressure" and set a timer for 15 minutes on "high."
7. Release pressure naturally, open the lid and select "broil."
8. Set timer for 8 minutes at 375 degrees F.
9. Serve and enjoy.

Per Serving: Calories 506, Fat 36.3 g, Carbs 7.6 g, Protein 35.9 g

Mustard Pork Chops

You definitely will love it! They are a favorite dinner recipe for many. With the touch of garlic clove, lemon and lime juice, this recipe has such a tantalizing taste that you will not want to stop eating midway until you finish.

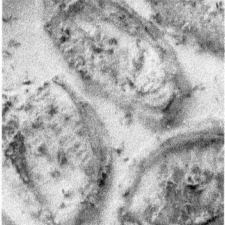

Prep time 15 minutes/ Cook time 30 minutes/ Serves 4

Ingredients:
- 2 tablespoons butter
- 2 tablespoons Dijon mustard
- 4 pork chops
- Salt and black pepper, to taste

- 1 tablespoon fresh rosemary, coarsely chopped

Directions
1. Marinate chops with Dijon mustard, rosemary, salt, pepper and set aside for 2 hours.
2. Place pork chops, butter in a pot of Ninja Foodi.
3. Close the lid and select "pressure."
4. Set timer for 30 minutes on "Lo: Md."
5. Release pressure naturally, open the lid and serve.

Per Serving: Calories 315, Fat 26.1 g, Carbs 1 g, Protein 18.4 g

Spicy Pork Ribs

Have you always wanted to make your own Pork Ribs? Well here is your chance. This recipe is very easy to make, it takes less than one hour to make, and your ribs are ready.

Prep time 10 minutes/ Cook time 34 minutes/ Serves 4

Ingredients:
- 3 lbs. pork ribs, cut into thirds
- ¾ cup of water
- 1 tablespoon erythritol
- 1 teaspoon oregano, dried
- 1 teaspoon red chili powder
- ½ teaspoon garlic powder
- ¾ cup tomato paste
- 1 teaspoon dried thyme
- 1 teaspoon sweet paprika
- ½ teaspoon cayenne pepper
- ½ teaspoon onion powder
- Salt and pepper to taste

Directions
1. Rub pork ribs with salt, pepper.
2. Place water in the pot of Ninja Foodi.
3. Place ribs in "cook and crisp basket" and place this basket in the pot.
4. Close the lid and set the valve to seal.
5. Select "pressure" and set timer 19 minutes on "high."
6. Quickly release the pressure.
7. Open the lid of the Ninja Foodi.
8. Select "air crisp" and set the timer for 15 minutes at 400 degrees F.
9. Take a bowl and add the remaining ingredients in it.
10. Open the lid and coat chops with sauce and close the lid for 5 minutes.
11. Serve and enjoy.

Per Serving: Calories 977, Fat 60.8 g, Carbs 13.5 g, Protein 92.6 g

Pork Chops with Cabbage

The meal takes about 22 minutes to make; 10 minutes preparation time and 12 minutes for the cooking. It is definitely you can make on a busy day, and before you know it, you are out of the kitchen.

Prep time 10 minutes/ Cook time 12 minutes/ Serves 6
Ingredients:
- 2 lbs. pork chops, boneless
- 1 cabbage head, cut in chunks
- ¼ cup butter
- 2 cups chicken broth
- Salt and pepper to taste

Directions
1. Season pork chops with salt and pepper.
2. Place pork chops in the pot of Ninja Foodi, followed by cabbage, broth, and butter.
3. Close the lid and select "pressure."
4. Set the timer to 12 minutes on "high."
5. Do a natural release and open the lid.
6. Serve and enjoy.

Per Serving: Calories 594, Fat 45.8 g, Carbs 7.2 g, Protein 37.2 g

BBQ Pork Chops

This is a recipe with a lot of flavor, and you are up for a treat with it. Pork chops are very delicious and are loved by almost everyone that has ever tasted them.

Prep time 10 minutes/ Cook time 16 minutes/ Serves 6
Ingredients:
- 6 lbs. pork chops
- ½ cup sugar-free BBQ sauce
- Salt and pepper to taste

Directions:
1. Take a meat tenderizer and tenderize the chops.
2. Season chops with salt and pepper.
3. Take a bowl and add sauce, chops and mix well.
4. Refrigerate chops for 6-8 hours.
5. Arrange chops on "coo and crisp basket" and this basket in the Ninja Foodi.
6. Close the lid and select "air crisp."
7. Set timer for 16 minutes at 355 degrees F.
8. Flip chops halfway through.
9. Press stop, open the lid and serve.

Per Serving: Calories 1472, Fat 112.7 g, Carbs 4 g, Protein 101.9 g

Seasoned Pork Tenderloin

It is perfect for the Ninja Foodi, and comes out just as perfect as the Instant Pot or any other pressure cooker.

Prep time 10 minutes/ Cook time 29 minutes/ Serves 3

Ingredients:
- 1 lb. pork tenderloin
- 2 tablespoons Mrs. Dash seasoning
- 2 cups beef broth
- 2 tablespoons olive oil
- Salt and pepper to taste

Directions
1. Season pork with seasoning, salt, and pepper.
2. Turn on the Ninja Foodi and select sauté.
3. All oil and sauté for 3 minutes.
4. Add pork and cook for 2 minutes on each side.
5. Transfer pork on a plate.
6. Pour broth in the pot of Ninja Foodi.
7. Place trivet in the pot and pork on the trivet.
8. Close the lid and select "bake/roast."
9. Set the timer to 25 minutes at 350 degrees F and press stop.
10. Open the lid and transfer pork tenderloin on the cutting board.

Per Serving: Calories 322, Fat 15.6 g, Carbs 0.6 g, Protein 42.8 g

Spicy Pork Loin

A bit of protein, a bit of good fat, and a bit of vitamins is what you have right here in this recipe. You can make some more steamed veggies to enjoy the sauce with or have it with a side of steamed green.

Prep time 10 minutes/ Cook time 38 minutes/ Serves 10

Ingredients:
- 3 lbs. pork loin, boneless
- 2 teaspoons smoked paprika
- 1 teaspoon garlic powder
- 2 cups beef broth
- Olive oil
- Salt and pepper to taste

Directions
1. Grease the pot of Ninja Foodi and select sauté.
2. Add oil, paprika, garlic, pork loin and cook for 3-4 minutes on each side.
3. Season beef with salt and pepper.
4. Transfer pork on a plate.
5. Pour broth in a pot of Ninja Foodi.
6. Place pork on trivet and trivet in the pot.
7. Close the lid and set the valve to seal.
8. Select "pressure" and set the timer for 30 minutes on "high."

9. Do a natural release for 5 minutes and then quick release, open the lid.
10. Transfer pork on a cutting board, cut them in slices and serve.

Per Serving: Calories 331, Fat 19 g, Carbs 0.4 g, Protein 37.3 g

Shredded Pork Shoulder

It is amazing how this shoulder cooks in very little time than expected and this should be the case when cooking meat to not kill the nutrients in the food.

Prep time 10 minutes/ Cook time 38 minutes/ Serves 6

Ingredients:
- 2 lbs. pork shoulder, boneless and cubed
- 3 tablespoons lemon juice
- 2 teaspoons lemon zest
- ½ teaspoon red chili powder
- ½ cup chicken broth
- 6 garlic cloves, crushed
- 1 teaspoon dried oregano
- 1 teaspoon ground cumin
- ½ onion, peeled
- 1 tablespoon parsley, chopped
- Salt and pepper to taste

Directions
1. Place pork shoulder, lemon juice, lemon zest, garlic, chili powder, oregano, cumin, salt, pepper in the pot and stir to combine.
2. Top with onion, broth and close the lid.
3. Select "pressure" and set the timer to 20 minutes at "high."
4. Do a quick release and open the lid.
5. Remove onion and shred the meat.
6. Select sauté and sauté for 10 minutes on "Md:Hi".
7. Close the lid and select "broil."
8. Broil for 8 minutes and open the lid.
9. Serve with parsley and enjoy.

Per Serving: Calories 458, Fat 32.7 g, Carbs 2.7 g, Protein 36.1 g

Apple and Onion Topped Pork Chops

This recipe is a combination of sweetness and sharpness but in all, it is SUPER tasty.

Prep time 5 minutes/ Cook time 25 minutes/ Serves 3

Ingredients:
- 1 small onion, sliced
- 2 tbsp olive oil

- 1 tbsp apple cider vinegar
- 2 tsp thyme
- ¼ tsp brown sugar
- 1 cup sliced apples
- 2 tsp rosemary
- ¼ tsp smoked paprika
- 1 tbsp olive oil
- 3 pork chops
- 1 tbsp apple cider vinegar
- Salt and pepper, to taste

Directions:
1. Preheat the Ninja Air fryer to 350 degrees F.
2. Place all topping ingredients in a baking dish, and then in the air fryer.
3. Cook for 4 minutes on Air Fry mode.
4. Meanwhile, place the pork chops in a bowl.
5. Add olive oil, vinegar, paprika, and season with salt and pepper.
6. Stir to coat them well. Remove the topping from the dish.
7. Add the pork chops in the dish and cook for 10 minutes on Air Fry mode.
8. Place the topping on top, return to the air fryer and cook for 5 more minutes.

Per Serving: Calories 434, Carbs 30g, Fat 33g, Protein 27g

The Crispiest Roast Pork

This recipe is good for a family get-together dinner. If you like it a little drizzle on steamed veggies is amazing. Then, with a broccoli mash, words can't explain the taste, and with rice, girl, you'll be up for a fantastic time.

Prep time 10 minutes/ Cook time 50 minutes/ Serves 4

Ingredients:
- 4 pork tenderloins
- 1 tsp five spice seasoning
- ½ tsp white pepper
- ¾ tsp garlic powder
- 1 tsp salt
- Cooking spray

Directions:
1. Place the pork, white pepper, garlic powder, five seasoning, and salt into a bowl and toss to coat.
2. Leave to marinate at room temperature for 30 minutes.
3. Preheat the Ninja air fryer to 360 degrees F.
4. Place the pork into the air fryer basket, greased with cooking spray and cook for 20 minutes. After 10 minutes, turn the tenderloins.
5. Serve hot.

Per Serving: Calories 752, Carbs 22g, Fat 69g, Protein 55g

Philippine-Style Pork Chops

Yup! Something that doesn't take a struggle of the teeth to enjoy. This recipe takes a short time and the pork is so tender.

Prep time 15 minutes/ Cook time 2 hours 20 minutes/ Serves 6
Ingredients:
- 2 lb. pork chops
- 2 bay leaves
- 2 tbsp soy sauce
- 5 garlic cloves, coarsely chopped
- 1 tbsp peppercorns
- 1 tbsp peanut oil
- 1 tsp salt

Directions:
1. Combine the bay leaves, soy sauce, garlic, salt, peppercorns, and oil, in a bowl.
2. Rub the mixture onto the meat. Wrap the pork with a plastic foil and refrigerate for 2 hours. Preheat the Ninja Air fryer to 350 degrees F.
3. Place the pork in the air fryer and cook for 10 minutes on Air Fry mode. Increase the temperature to 370 F, flip the chops, and cook for another 10 minutes. Discard bay leaves before serving.

Per Serving: Calories 712, Carbs 1.2g, Fat 82g, Protein 14g

Honey Barbecue Pork Ribs

Really simple recipe, but filled with a lot of good nutrients. It cooks in about half an hour, so you needn't worry when you get trapped in hunger. Put everything together in the pot, hit start, and get your plate ready.

Prep time 15 minutes/ Cook time 4 hours 35 minutes/ Serves 2
Ingredients:
- 1 lb. pork ribs
- ½ tsp five spice powder
- 1 tsp salt
- 3 garlic cloves, chopped
- 1 tsp black pepper
- 1 tsp sesame oil
- 1 tbsp honey, plus more for brushing
- 4 tbsp barbecue sauce
- 1 tsp soy sauce

Directions:
1. Chop the ribs into smaller pieces and place in a large bowl.
2. In a separate bowl, whisk together all of the other ingredients.
3. Add to the bowl with the pork, and mix until the pork is thoroughly coated.
4. Cover the bowl, place it in the fridge, and let it marinade for about 4 hours.
5. Preheat the Ninja Air fryer to 350 degrees F.
6. Place the ribs in the basket of the air fryer. Cook for 15 minutes on Air Fry mode.
7. After, brush the ribs with some honey and cook for 15 more minutes.

Per Serving: Calories 940, Carbs 22g, Fat 69g, Protein 55g

Char Siew Pork Ribs

Such a quick but taste-enhancing way to cook pork. The pork chops are that kind you look forward to having after a hard day of work. It is rewarding of your efforts, and the whole family will dine well to.

Prep time 15 minutes/ Cook time 4 hours 55 minutes/ Serves 6

Ingredients:
- 2 lb. pork ribs
- 2 tbsp char siew sauce
- 2 tbsp minced ginger
- 2 tbsp hoisin sauce
- 2 tbsp sesame oil
- 1 tbsp honey
- 4 garlic cloves, minced
- 1 tbsp soy sauce

Directions:
1. Whisk together all marinade ingredients, in a small bowl.
2. Coat the ribs well with the mixture. Place in a container with a lid, and refrigerate for 4 hours. Preheat the Ninja Air fryer to 330 degrees F.
3. Place the ribs in the basket but do not throw away the liquid from the container.
4. Cook for 40 minutes on Air Fry mode.
5. Stir in the liquid, increase the temperature to 350 F, and cook for 10 more minutes.

Per Serving: Calories 722, Carbs 15g, Fat 37g, Protein 33g

CHAPTER 7: VEGETABLES 20 RECIPES

Chives Beets and Carrots

Super packed with richness: proteins, vitamins, and healthy fats. This recipe is so filling and delicious.

Prep time 5 minutes/ Cook time 20 minutes/ Serves 4
Ingredients:
- 1-pound beets, peeled and roughly cubed
- 1-pound baby carrots, peeled
- Salt and black pepper to the taste
- 2 tablespoons olive oil
- 1 tablespoon chives, minced

Directions:
1. In a bowl, mix the beets with the carrots and the other ingredients and toss.
2. Put the beets and carrots in the Foodie's basket, cook on Air Crisp at 390 degrees F for 20 minutes, divide between plates and serve.

Per Serving: calories 150, fat 4.5g, carbs 7.3g, protein 3.6g

Minty Radishes

You can't get enough of the creamy, tasty goodness that this recipe has to offer. You've just got to love-it!

Prep time 5 minutes/ Cook time 15 minutes/ Serves 4
Ingredients:
- 1-pound radishes, halved
- salt and black pepper
- 2 tablespoons balsamic vinegar
- 2 tablespoon mint, chopped
- 2 tablespoons olive oil

Directions:
1. In your Foodi's basket, combine the radishes with the vinegar and the other ingredients, and cook on Air Crisp at 380 degrees F for 15 minutes.
2. Divide the radishes between plates and serve.

Per Serving: calories 170, fat 4.5g, carbs 7.4g, protein 4.6g

Carrots and Walnuts Salad

Fun fact here: carrots, and walnuts are given an aromatic kick. With this, your meaty plates just got a lot more pleasant. Make sure to cook them not to be too wilted so that you can enjoy some crunch with as you bite on.

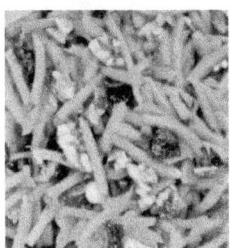

Prep time 5 minutes/ Cook time 15 minutes/ Serves 4
Ingredients:
- 4 carrots, roughly shredded
- ½ cup walnuts, sliced
- 3 tablespoons balsamic vinegar
- 1 cup chicken stock
- Salt and black pepper to the taste
- 1 tablespoon olive oil

Directions:
1. In your Foodi, mix the carrots with the vinegar and the other ingredients except the walnuts, put the pressure lid on and cook on High for 15 minutes.
2. Release the pressure fast for 5 minutes, divide the mix between plates and serve with the walnuts sprinkled on top.

Per Serving: calories 120, fat 4.5g, carbs 5.3g, protein 1.3g

Soy Kale

Any time is the best time to enjoy some tasty soy kale. It will satisfy hunger pangs at the right moments.

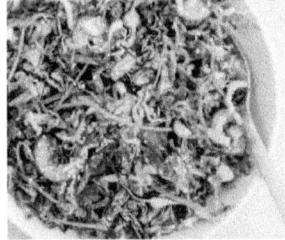

Prep time 5 minutes/ Cook time 15 minutes/ Serves 4
Ingredients:
- 2 pounds kale, torn
- ½ cup soy sauce
- 1 teaspoon honey
- 2 teaspoons olive oil
- ½ teaspoon garlic powder
- Salt and black pepper

Directions:
1. In your Foodi, combine the kale with the soy sauce and the other ingredients, put the pressure lid on and cook on High for 15 minutes.
2. Release the pressure fast for 5 minutes, divide everything between plates and serve.

Per Serving: calories 120, fat 3.5g, carbs 3.3g, protein 1.1g

Chili Eggplant and Kale

This dish poses as a faux lasagna but is cheesy tasty to the core. In 15 minutes or less, it gets ready and is perfect to enjoy by itself, or you may add it as a side to a meat dish.

Prep time 5 minutes/ Cook time 15 minutes/ Serves 4
Ingredients:
- Juice of 1 lime
- 1-pound eggplant, roughly cubed
- 1 cup kale, torn
- A pinch of salt and black pepper
- ½ teaspoon chili powder
- ½ cup chicken stock
- 3 tablespoons olive oil

Directions:
1. Set the Foodi on Sauté mode, add the oil, heat it up, add the eggplant and sauté for 2 minutes.
2. Add the kale and the rest of the ingredients, put the pressure lid on and cook on and cook on High for 13 minutes.
3. Release the pressure fast for 5 minutes, divide the mix between plates and serve.

Per Serving: calories 110, fat 3g, carbs 4.3g, protein 1.1g

Lime Broccoli and Cauliflower

Make this crunchy recipe as often as you can to go with the different sauces and meat dishes that are shared here.

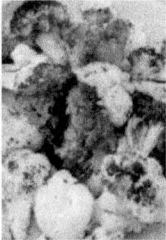

Prep time 10 minutes/ Cook time 15 minutes/ Serves 4
Ingredients:
- 2 cups broccoli florets
- 1 cup cauliflower florets
- 2 tablespoons lime juice
- 1 tablespoon avocado oil
- 1/3 cup tomato sauce
- 2 teaspoons ginger, grated
- 2 teaspoons garlic, minced
- 1 tablespoon chives, chopped

Directions:
1. Set the Foodi on Sauté mode, add the oil, heat it up, add the garlic and the ginger and sauté for 2 minutes.
2. Add the broccoli, cauliflower and the rest of the ingredients, put the pressure lid on and cook on High for 13 minutes.
3. Release the pressure naturally for 10 minutes, divide everything between plates and serve.

Per Serving: calories 118, fat 1.5g, carbs 4.3g, protein 6g

Garlic Red Bell Peppers Mix

This tasty Garlic Red Bell Peppers Mix can be enjoyed at any time. I reckon it will satisfy hunger pangs at the right moments.

Prep time 5 minutes/ Cook time 16 minutes/ Serves 4
Ingredients:
- 1-pound red bell peppers, cut into wedges
- ½ teaspoon curry powder
- ½ cup tomato sauce
- Salt and black pepper to the taste
- 1 tablespoon olive oil
- 2 garlic cloves, minced
- 1 tablespoon parsley, chopped

Directions:
1. Put the reversible rack in the Foodi, add the baking pan inside and grease it with the oil.
2. Add the peppers, curry powder and the other ingredients except the parsley, toss a bit and cook on Baking mode at 380 degrees F for 16 minutes.
3. Divide between plates and serve with the parsley sprinkled on top.

Per Serving: calories 150, fat 3.5g, carbs 3.1g, protein 1.2g

Zucchinis and Spinach Mix

This recipe is a great meal for a date night. It is quite easy and quick to prepare. It is full of flavor and you and your partner will enjoy it all the way!

Prep time 5 minutes/ Cook time 17 minutes/ Serves 4
Ingredients:
- 2 zucchinis, sliced
- 1-pound baby spinach
- ½ cup tomato sauce
- Salt and black pepper
- 1 tablespoon avocado oil
- 1 red onion, chopped
- 1 tablespoon sweet paprika
- ½ teaspoon garlic powder
- ½ teaspoon chili powder

Directions:
1. Set the Foodi on Sauté, add the oil, heat it up, add the onion and sauté for 2 minutes.
2. Add the zucchinis, spinach, and the other ingredients, put the pressure lid on and cook on High for 15 minutes.
3. Release the pressure fast for 5 minutes, divide everything between plates and serve.

Per Serving: calories 130, fat 5.5g, carbs 3.3g, protein 1g

Potatoes and Lemon Sauce

Are you craving for special-made potatoes? Then, this is the recipe you have been looking for. This recipe will satisfy your hungry family and is full of nutrients.

Prep time 5 minutes/ Cook time 15 minutes/ Serves 4
Ingredients:
- 1-pound gold potatoes, peeled and cut into wedges
- 1 tablespoon dill, chopped
- 1 tablespoon lemon zest, grated
- Juice of ½ lemon
- 2 tablespoons butter, melted
- Salt and black pepper to the taste

Directions:
1. Set the Foodi on Sauté mode, add the butter, melt it, add the potatoes and brown for 5 minutes.
2. Add the lemon zest and the other ingredients, set the machine on Air Crisp and cook at 390 degrees F for 10 minutes.
3. Divide everything between plates and serve.

Per Serving: calories 122, fat 3.3g, carbs 3g. protein 2g

Lemony Leeks and Carrots

The ingredients of this recipe nourishing and simple. They also taste so well. It only has few ingredients which also means that it can be fixed easily and quickly.

Prep time 5 minutes/ Cook time 15 minutes/ Serves 4
Ingredients:
- 2 leeks, roughly sliced
- 2 carrots, sliced
- 1 teaspoon ginger powder
- 1 teaspoon garlic powder
- ½ cup chicken stock
- Salt and black pepper to the taste
- 2 tablespoons lemon juice
- 2 tablespoons olive oil
- ½ tablespoon balsamic vinegar

Directions:
1. In your Foodi, combine the leeks with the carrots and the other ingredients, put the pressure lid on and cook on High for 15 minutes.
2. Release the pressure fast for 5 minutes, divide the mix between plates and serve.

Per Serving: calories 133, fat 3.4g, carbs 5g, protein 2.1g

Sesame Radish and Leeks

Sesame Radish and Leeks recipe is filled with lots of flavors. It is easy and quick to make as you need only 15 minutes to cook it! You will enjoy its good taste and healthy nutrients.

Prep time 5 minutes/ Cook time 15 minutes/ Serves 4
Ingredients:
- 2 leeks, sliced
- ½ pound radishes, sliced
- 2 scallions, chopped
- 2 tablespoons black sesame seeds
- 1/3 cup chicken stock
- 1 tablespoon ginger, grated
- 1 tablespoon chives, minced

Directions:
1. In your Foodi, combine the leeks with the radishes and the other ingredients, put the pressure lid on and cook on High for 15 minutes more.
2. Release the pressure fast for 5 minutes, divide everything between plates and serve.

Per Serving: calories 112, fat 2g, carbs 4.2g, protein 2g

Radish and Apples Mix

This mix is good and can be taken as a snack and a main meal. You will love it.

Prep time 5 minutes/ Cook time 15 minutes/ Serves 4
Ingredients:
- 1-pound radishes, roughly cubed
- 2 green apples, cored and cut into wedges
- ¼ cup chicken stock
- 2 spring onions, chopped
- 3 tablespoons tomato paste
- Juice of 1 lime
- Cooking spray
- 1 tablespoon cilantro, chopped

Directions:
1. In your Foodi, combine the radishes with the apples and the other ingredients, put the pressure lid on and cook on High for 15 minutes.
2. Release the pressure fast for 5 minutes, divide everything between plates and serve.

Per Serving: calories 122, fat 5g, carbs 4.5g, protein 3g

Lime Cabbage and Bacon

Bacon tastes great. And now with the introduction of lime cabbage, it tastes even more sweet.

Prep time 5 minutes/ Cook time 20 minutes/ Serves 4
Ingredients:
- 4 cups red cabbage, shredded
- ¼ cup veggie stock
- A pinch of salt and black pepper
- 1 tablespoon olive oil
- 1 cup canned tomatoes, crushed
- Zest of 1 lime, grated
- 2 ounces bacon, cooked and crumbled

Directions:
1. Put the reversible rack in the Foodi, add the baking pan inside and grease it with the oil.
2. Add the cabbage, the stock and the other ingredients into the pan and cook on Baking mode at 380 degrees F for 20 minutes.
3. Divide the mix between plates and serve.

Per Serving: calories 144, fat 3g, carbs 4.5g, protein 4.4g

Napa Cabbage and Carrots

This recipe is easily fixed and takes just 20 minutes to cook and 5 minutes for preparation.

Prep time 5 minutes/ Cook time 20 minutes/ Serves 4
Ingredients:
- 1 Napa cabbage, shredded
- 2 carrots, sliced
- 2 tablespoons olive oil
- 1 red onion, chopped
- Salt and black pepper to the taste
- 2 tablespoons sweet paprika
- ½ cup tomato sauce

Directions:
1. Set the Foodi on Sauté mode, add the oil, heat it up, add the onion and sauté for 5 minutes.
2. Add the carrots, the cabbage and the other ingredients, toss, put the pressure lid on and cook on High for 15 minutes.
3. Release the pressure fast for 5 minutes, divide everything between plates and serve.

Per Serving: calories 140, fat 3.4g, carbs 1.2g, protein 3.5 g

Parsley Kale and Leeks

This recipe is perfectly cooked to bring out the sweet flavors and healthy nutrients in its ingredients. It is filled with lots of flavor and healthy fats and the texture is just right.

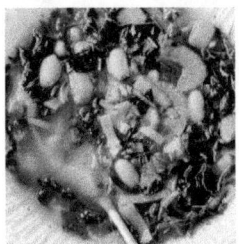

Prep time 5 minutes/ Cook time 15 minutes/ Serves 4
Ingredients:
- 1-pound kale, torn
- 2 leeks, sliced
- 2 tablespoons balsamic vinegar
- 1 tablespoon parsley, chopped
- Salt and black pepper to the taste
- 2 shallots, chopped
- ½ cup tomato sauce

Directions:
1. In your Foodi, combine the kale with the leeks and the other ingredients, put the pressure lid on and cook on High for 15 minutes.
2. Release the pressure fast for 5 minutes, divide the mix between plates and serve.

Per Serving: calories 100, fat 2g, carbs 3.4g, protein 4g

Balsamic Cabbage and Endives

This recipe is tasty, fresh and so delicious. It is also easy to make and has lots of nutrients which are good for you. It can made for your family or your guests.

Prep time 5 minutes/ Cook time 15 minutes/ Serves 4
Ingredients:
- 1 green cabbage head, shredded
- 2 endives, trimmed and sliced lengthwise
- Salt and black pepper to the taste
- 1 tablespoon olive oil
- 2 shallots, chopped
- ½ cup chicken stock
- 1 tablespoon sweet paprika
- 1 tablespoon balsamic vinegar

Directions:
1. Set the Foodi on Sauté mode, add the oil, heat it up, add the shallots and sauté for 2 minutes.
2. Add the cabbage, the endives and the other ingredients, put the pressure lid on and cook on High for 13 minutes.
3. Release the pressure fast for 5 minutes, divide the mix between plates and serve.

Per Serving: calories 120, fat 2g, carbs 3.3g, protein 4

Creamy Kale

It is amazingly delicious and filled with lots of flavors. it can be eaten with quite a range of raw veggies therefore making it versatile.

Prep time 5 minutes/ Cook time 15 minutes/ Serves 4
Ingredients:
- 1 tablespoon lemon juice
- 2 tablespoons balsamic vinegar
- 1-pound kale, torn
- 1 tablespoon ginger, grated
- 1 garlic clove, minced
- 2 tablespoons olive oil
- 1 cup heavy cream
- A pinch of salt and black pepper
- 2 tablespoons chives, chopped

Directions:
1. Set the Foodi on Sauté mode, add the oil, heat it up, add the garlic and the ginger and sauté for 2 minutes.
2. Add the kale, lemon juice and the other ingredients, put the pressure lid on and cook on High for 13 minutes.
3. Release the pressure fast for 5 minutes, divide between plates and serve.

Per Serving: calories 130, fat 2g, carbs 3.4g, protein 2g

Kale and Parmesan

This recipe is very simple and easy to prepare. It is a delicious recipe that has lots of flavors. It is very nutritious and a good protein source.

Prep time 5 minutes/ Cook time 15 minutes/ Serves 4
Ingredients:
- 1-pound kale, torn
- 2 tablespoons parmesan, grated
- 1 red onion, sliced
- 1 cup bacon, cooked and chopped
- ½ cup chicken stock
- 1 tablespoon olive oil
- A pinch of salt and black pepper
- 1 tablespoon balsamic vinegar

Directions:
1. Set the Foodi on Sauté mode, add the oil, heat it up, add the onion and sauté for 2 minutes.
2. Add the kale and the other ingredients except the parmesan.
3. Sprinkle the cheese at the end, set the machine on Baking mode and cook at 380 degrees F for 12 minutes.
4. Divide everything into bowls and serve.

Per Serving: calories 130, fat 5g, carbs 3.4g, protein 6g

Pomegranate Radish Mix

Pomegranate Radish Mix is full of sweet flavor and takes only 8 minutes to cook which is not much time and therefore it be considered a quick fix.

Prep time 5 minutes/ Cook time 8 minutes/ Serves 4
Ingredients:
- 1-pound radishes, roughly cubed
- Salt and black pepper to the taste
- 2 garlic cloves, minced
- ½ cup chicken stock
- 2 tablespoons pomegranate juice
- ¼ cup pomegranate seeds

Directions:
1. In your Foodi, combine the radishes with the stock and the other ingredients, put the pressure lid on and cook on High for 8 minutes.
2. Release the pressure fast for 5 minutes, divide everything between plates and serve.

Per Serving: calories 133, fat 2.3g, carbs 2.4g, protein 2g

Pine Nuts Okra and Leeks

It is made few ingredients and is very delicious. If you are craving a perfect veggie snack, then this is the perfect one for you. It is easy to make and you will love this mouthwatering delicacy.

Prep time 5 minutes/ Cook time 12 minutes/ Serves 4
Ingredients:
- 1-pound okra, trimmed
- 2 leeks, sliced
- Salt and black pepper to the taste
- 1 cup tomato sauce
- ¼ cup pine nuts, toasted
- 1 tablespoon cilantro, chopped

Directions:
1. In your Foodi, mix the okra with the leeks and the other ingredients except the cilantro, put the pressure lid on and cook on High for 12 minutes.
2. Release the pressure fast for 5 minutes, divide the okra mix into bowls and serve with the cilantro sprinkled on top.

Per Serving: calories 146, fat 3g, carbs 4g, protein 3g

CHAPTER 8: DESSERTS & APPETIZERS 20 RECIPES

Tapioca Pudding

Wondering what to serve for the next homemade brunch? Wonder no more because this is the perfect recipe that!

Prep time 15 minutes/ Cook time 32 minutes/ Serves 4

Ingredients:
- 1 cup tapioca pearls
- 2 eggs
- 3 cups whole milk
- ¼ tsp salt
- ½ cup granulated sugar
- 1 tsp vanilla extract

Directions
1. In the inner pot, add the tapioca, milk, and salt.
2. Cover with the Pressure Lid and close the vent to Seal. Select Pressure, adjust to High, and set the timer to 5 minutes. Press Start to begin cooking.
3. After cooking, perform a natural pressure release for 15 minutes, then a quick pressure release to let out the remaining steam, and open the lid.
4. Beat the eggs in a medium bowl and mix in 2 tablespoons of the tapioca liquid until adequately mixed. Pour the mixture into the tapioca along with the sugar and vanilla.
5. Select Sear/Sauté mode, adjust to Medium, and choose Start/Stop to continue cooking the pudding while still mixing. Cook for 5 to 10 minutes.
6. Spoon the pudding into serving bowls, allow complete cooling, and chill for 1 hour.
7. Serve afterward.

Per Serving: Calories 526, Carbs 70.81g, Fats 17.19g, Protein 20.77g

New York Style Cheesecake

The New York Style Cheesecake is finger licking sweet despite it taking long to get ready.

Prep time 15 minutes/ Cook time 56 minutes/ Serves 4

Ingredients:
- 12 graham crackers
- 16 oz cream cheese, softened
- ½ cup sour cream
- 2 eggs
- 2 tbsp arrowroot starch
- 1 ½ tbsp brown sugar
- 2 tbsp melted salted butter
- 1 cup granulated sugar

- 1 tsp vanilla extract
- 2 pinches salt

Directions
1. Pour the graham crackers into a plastic bag and gently crush by pounding with a rolling pin.
2. Pour the biscuit into a medium bowl and mix in the brown sugar and butter. Spoon the mixture into a 7-inch springform pan and use a spoon to press the mixture to fit into the bottom of the pan.
3. Pour 1 cup of water into the inner pot. Fix in the Reversible Rack in the lower position and place the cake pan on top.
4. Close the Air Crisping Lid; select Air Crisp; adjust the temperature to 350°F and the time to 6 minutes. Press Start and bake until set. Remove the cake pan and allow the crust to cool.
5. In a large bowl, using an electric hand mixer, whisk the cream cheese and granulated sugar until smooth. Mix in the sour cream, eggs, arrowroot starch, vanilla, and salt.
6. Pour the filling onto the crust and use a spatula to spread evenly. Cover the pan with foil and place the cake pan on the rack.
7. Cover with the Pressure Lid and lock the vent to Seal. Select Pressure; adjust to High and the time to 25 minutes. Press Start.
8. After cooking, perform a natural pressure release for 10 minutes, and then a quick pressure release to let out any remaining pressure.
9. Carefully open the lid and remove the cheesecake from the pot. Remove the foil.
10. Allow the cake to rest for 10 to 15 minutes and then chill in the refrigerator for 3 to 4 hours.
11. Slice and serve when ready to enjoy.

Per Serving: Calories 745, Fats 53.39g, Carbs 41.37g, Protein 25.01g

Yellow Cake Pineapple Upside Down

These cakes are delicious recipes made with pineapple, and yellow cake mix. They are easy to prepare and very delicious.

Prep time 15 minutes/ Cook time 38 minutes/ Serves 4

Ingredients:
- 1 box yellow cake mix
- 1 cup pineapple slices
- 2 tbsp butter
- ¼ cup brown sugar

Directions
1. In a medium bowl, prepare the cake mix according to the instruction on box. Set aside.
2. Grease a 7-inch springform pan with butter, sprinkle the brown sugar at the bottom of the pan and arrange the pineapple slices on top. Pour the cake batter all over and cover the cake pan with foil.
3. Pour 1 ½ cups of water into the inner pot, fix in the Reversible Rack, and place the cake pan on top.
4. Cover with the Pressure Lid and lock the vent to Seal. Select Pressure; adjust to High and the time to 18 minutes. Press Start.
5. After cooking, perform a natural pressure release for 10 minutes, then a quick pressure release and carefully open the lid.
6. Carefully remove the cake pan, remove the foil, and allow cooling for 10 minutes.
7. Invert the cake onto a plate, slice, and serve.

Per Serving: Calories 670, Fats 13.01g, Carbs 133.44g, Protein 6.5g

Raspberry Cheesecake

This recipe is incredibly tasty. It has few ingredients and despite it taking almost an hour to get ready, it is awesome.

Prep time 20 minutes/ Cook time 56 minutes/ Serves 4

Ingredients:
- 12 graham crackers
- 16 oz cream cheese, softened
- 2 eggs
- ½ cup heavy cream
- 12 large fresh raspberries, mashed
- Items from your pantry:
- 2 tbsp brown sugar
- 2 tbsp melted butter
- 1 cup granulated sugar
- 2 tsp cinnamon powder
- 1 tsp vanilla extract
- 3 tbsp maple syrup

Directions
1. Pour the graham crackers into a plastic bag and gently crush by pounding a rolling pin on top.
2. Transfer the biscuit to a medium bowl and mix in the brown sugar and butter. Spoon the mixture into a 7-inch springform pan and using a spoon press the mixture to fit into the bottom of the pan.
3. Pour 1 cup of water into the inner pot. Fix in the Reversible Rack in the lower position and place the cake pan on top.
4. Close the Air Crisping Lid; select Air Crisp; adjust the temperature to 350°F and the time to 6 minutes. Press Start and bake until set. Remove the cake pan and allow the crust to cool.
5. In a large bowl, using an electric hand mixer, whisk the cream cheese and granulated sugar until smooth. Beat in the eggs, heavy cream, raspberries, cinnamon powder, vanilla extract, and maple syrup.
6. Pour the mixture onto the crust and use a spatula to spread evenly. Cover the pan with foil and place the cake pan on the rack.
7. Cover with the Pressure Lid and lock the vent to Seal. Select Pressure; adjust to High and the time to 25 minutes. Press Start.
8. After cooking, perform a natural pressure release for 10 minutes, and then a quick pressure release to let out any remaining pressure.
9. Carefully open the lid and remove the cheesecake from the pot. Remove the foil.
10. Allow the cake to rest for 10 to 15 minutes and then chill in the refrigerator for 3 to 4 hours.
11. Slice and serve when ready to enjoy.

Per Serving: Calories 679, Fats 48.43g, Carbs 51.29g, Protein 11.95g

Caramel Popcorns

Popcorns are a favorite for many when going for the movies. However, the caramel popcorns are tweaked to give it a different sweet taste that yo can't fail to love.

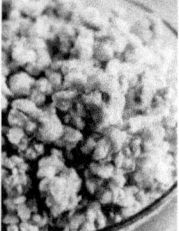

Prep time 10 minutes/ Cook time 9 minutes/ Serves 4

Ingredients:
- 1 cup sweet corn kernels
- 4 tbsp butter
- 3 tbsp brown sugar
- ¼ cup whole milk

Directions
1. Select Sear/Sauté mode, adjust to High, and choose Start/Stop to preheat the pot for 5 minutes.
2. Melt the butter in the inner pot and mix in the corn kernels.
3. Cover the pot with a regular glass pot lid that is large enough to cover the pot.
4. The corns will begin popping afterward. Cook until all the corns have popped, 5 minutes. Transfer to a large serving bowl after.
5. Wipe the inner pot clean and return to the base.
6. Still in Sear/Sauté mode, combine the brown sugar and milk in the inner pot. Cook with frequent stirring until the sugar dissolves and the sauce coats the back of the spoon, 3 to 4 minutes.
7. Drizzle the caramel sauce all over the popcorns and mix to coat well.
8. Cool for a few minutes and serve afterward.

Per Serving: Calories 189, Fats 14.06g, Carbs 14.14g, Protein 3.13g

Chocolate Crème de Pot

The Chocolate Crème de Pot Recipe has ingredients that are full of nutrients such as proteins and vitamins. This recipe has lots of flavors.

Prep time 15 minutes/ Cook time 19 minutes/ Serves 4

Ingredients:
- 1 ½ cups heavy cream
- 5 large egg yolks
- ¼ cup chocolate, melted
- Whipped cream for topping
- 1 tbsp chocolate sprinkles for garnishing
- ½ cup whole milk
- A pinch of salt
- ¼ cup caster sugar

Directions
1. Select Sear/Sauté mode, adjust to High, and choose Start/Stop to preheat the pot for 5 minutes.
2. Pour the heavy cream and milk into the inner pot and allow boiling.
3. Meanwhile, in a medium bowl, beat the egg yolks, salt, and sugar until well combined.
4. Gradually, whisk the egg mixture into the cream until well mixed. Also, stir in the melted chocolate and cook until thickened, 2 to 3 minutes.
5. Spoon the mixture into 4 medium ramekins and set side. Clean the inner pot and return to the base.
6. Pour 1 cup of water into the inner pot, fix in the Reversible Rack in the lower position in the inner pot and arrange 3 ramekins on the rack making sure that their edges touch each other to make a stand for the last ramekin. Place the fourth ramekin on top.
7. Cover with the Pressure Lid and lock the vent to Seal. Select Pressure; adjust to High and the time to 6 minutes. Press Start.
8. After cooking, perform a natural pressure release for 10 minutes, then a quick pressure release to let out any remaining pressure, and open the lid.
9. Use tongs to carefully remove the cups onto a flat surface and cool completely. Chill further in the refrigerator for at least 6 hours.
10. To serve, top the dessert with some whipping cream and decorate with the chocolate sprinkles.

Per Serving: Calories 394, Carbs 32.62g, Fats 26.88g, Protein 6.28g

Apricots Dulche de Leche

This recipe is finger-licking good and will leave you wanting more. So, don't just make little of it.

Prep time 10 minutes/ Cook time 55 minutes/ Serves 4
Ingredients:
- 2 cups sweetened condensed milk
- 4 apricots, halved, cored, and sliced

Directions
1. Divide the condensed milk into 4 medium ramekins.
2. Pour 2 cups of water into the inner pot, fix in the Reversible Rack in the lower position, and place the ramekins on top.
3. Cover with the Pressure Lid and lock the vent to Seal. Select Pressure; adjust to High and the time to 25 minutes. Press Start to cook.
4. After cooking, perform a natural pressure release for 30 minutes, and then a quick pressure release to let out any remaining pressure, and open the lid.
5. Remove the ramekins onto a flat surface and allow complete cooling.
6. After, use a fork to whisk the mixture until creamy and then, chill in the refrigerator for 1 hour.
7. To serve, top with the apricots and enjoy.

Per Serving: Calories 108, Fats 4.02g, Carbs 14.42g, Protein 4.06g

Blackberry Cobbler

Blackberry is loved by many and I guess you love it too. Try it today and you won't stop making it.

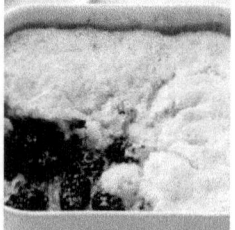

Prep time 15 minutes/ Cook time 15 minutes/ Serves 4
Ingredients:
- 4 cups fresh blackberries
- 2 tbsp + ¾ cup plain flour, divided
- ½ cup + ¼ cup brown sugar, divided
- ¼ tsp nutmeg powder
- ½ tsp cinnamon powder
- 1 tsp vanilla extract
- 1 ½ tsp salt, divided
- ¼ cup water
- ½ tsp baking powder
- ½ tsp baking soda
- 3 tbsp butter, melted

Directions
1. In a large ramekin, mix the blackberries, 2 tbsp of flour, ½ cup of brown sugar, nutmeg, cinnamon, vanilla, ½ teaspoon of salt, and water. Set aside.

2. Pour 1 cup of water in the inner pot, fix in the Reversible Rack, and place the ramekin on top.
3. Cover with the Pressure Lid and lock the vent to Seal. Select Pressure; adjust to High and the time to 3 minutes. Press Start.
4. After cooking, perform a quick pressure release to let out the remaining steam, and open the lid.
5. In another bowl, mix the remaining flour, brown sugar, salt, baking powder, baking soda, and butter. Spoon the mixture over the blackberry mixture and spread evenly on top to cover the filling.
6. Close the Air Crisping Lid and select Bake/Roast; adjust the temperature to 325°F and the time to 12 minutes. Press Start.
7. After 8 minutes; check if the dough is cooking right and continue cooking.
8. When the timer is done, the topping should be lightly browned and cooked through. Allow cooling before slicing. Serve warm.

Per Serving: Calories 649, Fats 9.67g, Carbs 134.57g, Protein 9.96g

Mango Rice Pudding

The mango gives the pudding a sweet taste that makes it interesting. You will enjoy every scoop.

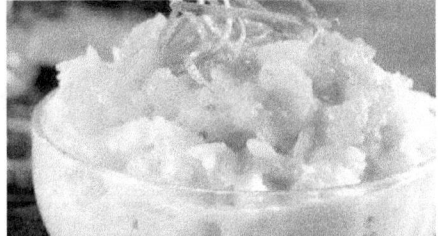

Prep time:10 minutes/ Cook time 15 minutes/ Serves 4

Ingredients:
- 1 cup jasmine rice
- 1 small mango, peeled and chopped into small bits
- Items from your pantry:
- 1 tsp vanilla extract
- ½ tsp nutmeg powder
- 2 cups whole milk
- 1 tbsp unsalted butter
- 1/3 cup granulated sugar
- A pinch of salt

Directions
1. Select Sear/Sauté mode, adjust to Medium High, and choose Start/Stop to preheat the pot for 5 minutes.
2. In the inner pot, mix the rice, mango, vanilla, nutmeg, milk, butter, sugar, and salt.
3. Cover with the Pressure Lid and lock the vent to Seal. Select Pressure; adjust to High and the time to 5 minutes. Press Start to cook.
4. After cooking, perform a natural pressure release for 10 minutes, then a quick pressure release to let out the steam, and open the lid.
5. Stir and adjust the taste with sugar.
6. Spoon into serving bowls and serve warm or chilled.

Per Serving: Calories 282, Carbs 45.09g, Fats 12.09g, Protein 8.03g,

Baked Stuffed Apples

Ever tried baked apples? They are crunchy and delicious at the same time. This incorporates chocolate and makes it very yummy!

Prep time 15 minutes/ Cook time 5 minutes/ Serves 4
Ingredients:
- 1/3 cup raisins
- 1/3 cup toasted pecans, chopped
- 1/3 cup dates, chopped
- 6 red apples, whole and cored
- 4 tbsp chocolate sauce for topping
- 2 tbsp brown sugar
- 4 tbsp butter
- 1 tbsp. cinnamon powder

Directions
1. Close the Air Crisping Lid and select Bake/Roast; adjust the temperature to 325°F and the time to 5 minutes. Press Start to preheat the lid.
2. In a medium bowl, mix the raisins, pecans, dates, brown sugar, butter, and cinnamon. Stuff the apples with the mixture.
3. After the lid has preheated, pour 1 cup of water into the inner pot, fix in the Reversible Rack in the lower position, and put the apples on top.
4. Close the Air Crisping Lid and select Bake/Roast; adjust the temperature to 325°F and the time to 5 minutes. Press Start.
5. Open the lid after cooking and use tongs to lift the apples onto serving plates carefully.
6. Swirl the chocolate sauce on the apples and serve immediately.

Per Serving: Calories 355, Fats 17.84g, Carbs 53.18g, Protein 2.16g

Sugar Cookie Pizza

This recipe in particular is something you can always make because it's no fuss and is fun for all ages.

Prep time 10 minutes/ Cook time 35 minutes/ Serves 6
Ingredients
- 22 ounces premade sugar cookie dough
- 5 tablespoons unsalted butter
- 1 package cream cheese
- 2 cups confectioners' sugar
- 1 teaspoon vanilla extract

Directions
1. Select bake/roast, set temperature to 325°F, and set time to 40 minutes. Select start/stop to begin. Let preheat for 5 minutes.
2. Press the cookie dough into the Ninja Multi-Purpose Pan in an even layer.
3. Once unit is preheated, place the pan on the Reversible Rack and place rack in the pot. Close crisping lid and cook for 35 minutes.
4. Once cooking is complete, remove the pan from the pot. Let cool in the refrigerator for 30 minutes.
5. In a large bowl, whisk together the butter, cream cheese, confectioners' sugar, and vanilla.
6. Once the cookie is chilled, carefully remove it from the pan. Using a spatula, spread the cream cheese mixture over cookie. Chill in the refrigerator for another 30 minutes.
7. Decorate with toppings of choice, such as sliced strawberries, raspberries, blueberries, blackberries, sliced kiwi, sliced mango, or sliced pineapple. Cut and serve.

Per serving: Calories: 791, Fat: 44g, Carbs: 92g, Protein: 7g

Sweet and Salty Bars

For this recipe, potato chips and pretzels are tossed in a sticky mixture of marshmallows and peanut butter and topped with chocolate. All of which comes together to create a dessert with the ultimate balance of sweet and salty.

Prep time 5 minutes/ Cook time 10 minutes/ Serves 12
Ingredients
- 1 cup light corn syrup
- 1 cup granulated sugar
- 1 teaspoon vanilla extract
- 1 bag mini marshmallows
- 1 cup crunchy peanut butter
- 1 bag potato chips with ridges, slightly crushed
- 1 cup pretzels, slightly crushed
- 1 bag hard-shelled candy-coated chocolates

Directions
1. Select sear/sauté and set temperature to md:hi. Select start/stop to begin. Let preheat for 5 minutes.
2. Add the corn syrup, sugar, and vanilla and stir until the sugar is melted.
3. Add the marshmallows and peanut butter and stir until the marshmallows are melted.
4. Add the potato chips and pretzels and stir until everything is evenly coated in the marshmallow mixture.
5. Pour the mixture into a 9-by-13-inch pan and place the chocolate candies on top, slightly pressing them in. Let cool, then cut into squares and serve.

Per serving: Calories: 585, Fats 21g, Carbs: 96g, Protein: 9g

Coconut Rice Pudding

Set up a topping station with fresh mango, toasted coconut, and nuts to really elevate this rice pudding to the next level and let your guests customize their dessert.

Prep time 5 minutes/ Cook time 8 minutes/ Serves 6
Ingredients
- ¾ cup arborio rice
- 1 can unsweetened full-fat coconut milk
- 1 cup milk
- 1 cup water
- ¾ cup granulated sugar
- ½ teaspoon vanilla extract

Directions
1. Rinse the rice under cold running water in a fine-mesh strainer.
2. Place the rice, coconut milk, milk, water, sugar, and vanilla in the pot and stir. Assemble pressure lid, making sure the pressure release valve is in the seal position.
3. Select pressure and set to hi. Set time to 8 minutes. Select start/stop to begin.

4. When pressure cooking is complete, allow pressure to naturally release for 10 minutes. After 10 minutes, quick release remaining pressure by moving the pressure release valve to the VENT position. Carefully remove lid when unit has finished releasing pressure.
5. Press a layer of plastic wrap directly on top of the rice (it should be touching) to prevent a skin from forming on top of the pudding. Let pudding cool to room temperature, then refrigerate overnight to set.
Per serving: Calories: 363, Fats 18g, Carbs: 50g, Protein: 5g

Cheese Babka

You can enjoy this babka for breakfast, dessert, or just a midday snack with a cup of tea or coffee.

Prep time 25 minutes/ Cook time 30 minutes/ Serves 8
Ingredients
For the dough
- 1 packet dry active yeast
- ¼ cup water, warmed to 110°F
- ¼ cup, plus ¼ teaspoon granulated sugar, divided
- 2 cups all-purpose flour
- 2 large eggs, divided
- ½ teaspoon kosher salt
- 3 tablespoons unsalted butter, at room temperature
- ¼ cup milk

For the filling
- 8 ounces cream cheese
- ¼ cup granulated sugar
- 1 tablespoon sour cream
- 1 tablespoon all-purpose flour
- ½ teaspoon vanilla extract
- Zest of 1 lemon
- Cooking spray
- All-purpose flour, for dusting
- 3 tablespoons water

Directions
To make the dough
1. In a small bowl, combine the yeast, warm water, and ¼ teaspoon of sugar. Let sit 10 minutes until foamy.
2. Place the flour, yeast mixture, remaining ¼ cup of sugar, 1 egg, salt, butter, and milk into the bowl of stand mixer. Using the dough hook attachment, mix on medium-low speed until the dough is smooth and elastic, about 10 minutes.

To make the filling
1. In a medium bowl, whisk together all the filling ingredients until smooth.

To make the babka
2. Spray the cooking pot with the cooking spray. Place the dough in the pot. Cover the dough with plastic wrap and let it rise in a warm place until doubled in size, about 1 hour.
3. Spray the Ninja Multi-Purpose Pan or 8-inch baking pan with cooking spray.
4. Turn the dough out onto a floured work surface. Punch down the dough. Using a rolling pin, roll it out into a 10-by-12-inch rectangle. Spread the cheese filling evenly on top of the dough. From the longer edge of the dough, roll it up like a jelly roll.
5. Cut the roll evenly into 12 pieces. Place each piece cut-side up in the prepared pan. The rolls should be touching but with visible gaps in between.

6. Beat the remaining egg with 1 teaspoon of water. Gently brush the tops of the rolls with this egg wash.
7. Place the remaining 3 tablespoons of water in the pot. Place the pan on the Reversible Rack, making sure the rack is in the lower position. Then place the rack with pan in the pot.
8. Select sear/sauté and set to LO. Select start/stop to begin.
9. After 5 minutes, select start/stop to turn off the heat. Let the rolls rise for another 15 minutes in the warm pot.
10. Remove the rack and pan from the pot. Close crisping lid.
11. Select bake/roast, set temperature to 325°F, and set time to 30 minutes. Select start/stop to begin. Let preheat for 5 minutes.
12. Place the rack with pan in the pot. Close lid and cook for 25 minutes.
13. Once cooking is complete, open lid and remove rack and pan. Let the babka completely cool before serving.

Per serving: Calories: 325, Fat: 16g, Carbs: 38g, Protein: 7g

Coconut Cream "Custard" Bars

This recipe is just as creamy, crunchy, and satisfying as you can imagine the custard would be. I think you'd be hard-pressed to find somebody who wouldn't agree.

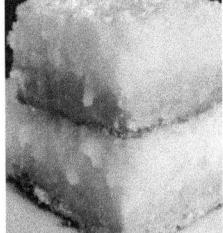

Prep time 8 minutes/ Cook time 20 minutes/ Serves 8

Ingredients
- 1¼ cups all-purpose flour
- 6 tablespoons unsalted butter, melted
- 2 tablespoons granulated sugar
- ½ cup unsweetened shredded coconut, divided
- ½ cup chopped almonds, divided
- Cooking spray
- 1 package instant vanilla pudding
- 1 cup milk
- 1 cup heavy, whipping cream
- 4 tablespoons finely chopped dark chocolate, divided

Directions
1. Select bake/roast, set temperature to 375°F, and set time to 15 minutes. Select start/stop to begin. Let preheat for 5 minutes.
2. To make the crust, combine the flour, butter, sugar, ¼ cup of coconut, and ¼ cup of almonds in a large bowl and stir until a crumbly dough form
3. Grease the Ninja Multi-Purpose Pan or an 8-inch round baking dish with cooking spray. Place the dough in the pan and press it into an even layer covering the bottom.
4. Once unit has preheated, place pan on Reversible Rack, making sure the rack is in the lower position. Open lid and place rack in pot. Close crisping lid. Reduce temperature to 325°F.
5. Place remaining ¼ cup each of almonds and coconut in a Ninja Loaf Pan or any small loaf pan and set aside.
6. When cooking is complete, remove rack with pan and let cool for 10 minutes.
7. Quickly place the loaf pan with coconut and almonds in the bottom of the pot. Close crisping lid.
8. Select air crisp, set temperature to 350°F, and set time to 10 minutes. Select start/stop to begin.
9. While the nuts and coconut toast, whisk together the instant pudding with the milk, cream, and 3 tablespoons of chocolate.
10. After 5 minutes, open lid and stir the coconut and almonds. Close lid and continue cooking for another 5 minutes.

11. When cooking is complete, open lid and remove pan from pot. Add the almonds and coconut to the pudding. Stir until fully incorporated. Pour this in a smooth, even layer on top of the crust.
12. Refrigerate for about 10 minutes. Garnish with the remaining 1 tablespoon of chocolate, cut into wedges, and serve.

Per serving: Calories: 476, Fat: 33g, Carbohydrates: 39g, Protein: 6g

Apple Crisp

Apple Crisp is a quick and easy alternative to apple pie, but it packs all of the warm cinnamon, spiced apple, and

buttery crumble crust you crave.

Prep time 15 minutes/ Cook time 20 minutes/ Serves 8

Ingredients
- 4 to 5 Granny Smith apples, peeled and cut into 1-inch cubes
- 1 tablespoon cornstarch
- ½ cup, plus 1 tablespoon water
- 2 teaspoons cinnamon, divided
- 1 teaspoon freshly squeezed lemon juice
- 5 tablespoons granulated sugar, divided
- ½ cup all-purpose flour
- ½ cup rolled oats
- ⅔ cup brown sugar
- ⅓ cup unsalted butter, melted

Directions
1. Place the apples in the Ninja Multi-Purpose Pan or a 1½-quart round ceramic baking dish.
2. In a small bowl, stir together the cornstarch, 1 tablespoon of water, 1 teaspoon of cinnamon, lemon juice, and 3 tablespoons of granulated sugar. Pour this mixture over the apples.
3. Place pan on Reversible Rack, making sure the rack is in the lower position. Cover the pan with aluminum foil. Pour the remaining ½ cup of water into the pot. Insert rack with pan in pot. Assemble pressure lid, making sure the pressure release valve is in the SEAL position.
4. Select pressure and set to HI. Set time to 0 minutes. Select start/stop to begin.
5. In a medium bowl, combine the flour, oats, brown sugar, butter, remaining 1 teaspoon of cinnamon, and remaining 2 tablespoons of granulated sugar until a crumble form.
6. When pressure cooking is complete, allow the pressure to naturally release for 10 minutes. After 10 minutes, quick release remaining pressure by moving the pressure release valve to the VENT position. Carefully remove lid when pressure has finished releasing.
7. Remove the foil and stir the fruit mixture. Evenly spread the crumble topping over the apples. Close crisping lid.
8. Select air crisp, set temperature to 375°F, and set time to 10 minutes. Select start/stop to begin.
9. Cooking is complete when the top is browned and the fruit is bubbling. Remove rack with the pan from the pot and serve.

Per serving: Calories: 261, Fat: 9g, Carbs: 46g, Protein: 2g

Brownie Bites

You may not believe how incredibly delicious the bites will turn out—nice and fudgy with no crumbs.

Prep time 5 minutes/ Cook time 45 minutes/ Serves 10
Ingredients
- Cooking spray
- 1 box brownie mix
- Confectioners' sugar
- Carmel sauce

Directions
1. Coat a silicone egg mold with nonstick cooking spray and set aside.
2. In a large bowl, prepare the brownie mix according to package instructions. Using a cookie scoop, transfer the batter to the prepared mold.
3. Place 1 cup water in the pot. Place the filled molds onto the Reversible Rack in the lower steam position, and lower into the pot.
4. Assemble the pressure lid, making sure the pressure release valve is in the seal position.
5. Select pressure and set to HI. Set the time to 45 minutes. Select start/stop to begin.
6. When pressure cooking is complete, allow the pressure to naturally release for 10 minutes. After 10 minutes, quick release any remaining pressure by moving the pressure release valve to the VENT position. Carefully remove the lid when the unit has finished releasing pressure
7. Carefully remove the mold from the cooker and let cool for 5 minutes
8. Flip the brownie onto a plate and garnish with confectioners' sugar and caramel sauce.

Per serving: Calories: 288, Fat: 5g, Carbs: 43g, Protein: 2g

Bacon Blondies

This recipe can be served with some vanilla ice cream on top as an extra contrast to the bacon.

Prep time 15 minutes/ Cook time 35 minutes/ Serves 6
Ingredients:
- 6 slices uncooked bacon, cut into ¼ slices
- 1½ cups unsalted butter, at room temperature
- 1 cup dark brown sugar
- 2 cups all-purpose flour
- Ice cream, for serving

Directions
1. Grease the Ninja Multi-Purpose Pan with butter.
2. Select sear/sauté and set to HI. Select start/stop to begin. Let preheat for 5 minutes.
3. Place the bacon in the pot. Cook, stirring frequently, for about 5 minutes, or until the fat is rendered and bacon starts to brown. Transfer the bacon to a paper towel-lined plate to drain. Wipe the pot clean of any remaining fat and return to unit.
4. In a medium bowl, beat the butter and brown sugar with a hand mixer until well incorporated. Slowly add in the flour and continue to beat until the flour is fully combined and a soft dough form. Next, fold the cooked bacon into the dough.

5. Press the dough into the prepared pan. Place pan on Reversible Rack, ensuring it is in the lower position. Lower rack into pot. Close crisping lid.
6. Select bake/roast, set temperature to 350°F, and set time to 25 minutes. Select start/stop to begin.
7. After 20 minutes, open lid and check for doneness by sticking a toothpick through the center of the dough. If it comes out clean, remove rack and pan from unit. If not, close lid and continue cooking.
8. When cooking is complete, remove rack and pan from unit. Let the blondies cool for about 30 minutes before serving with ice cream, if desired.

Per serving: Calories: 771, Fat: 54g, Carbs: 60g, Protein: 12g

Peanut Butter Pie

The combination of chocolate and peanut butter is a game changer. Whether you are going to a holiday party, summer cookout, or company potluck, this dessert will go over well.

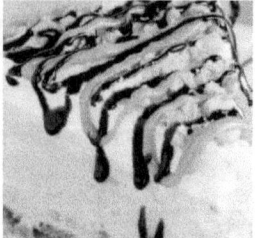

Prep time 10 minutes/ Cook time 30 minutes/ Serves 8

Ingredients
- 10 peanut butter cookies, crushed
- 3 tablespoons unsalted butter, melted
- 2 packages cream cheese
- ¾ cup granulated sugar
- 2 eggs
- ⅓ cup creamy peanut butter
- 10 chocolate peanut butter cups, chopped
- 2 cups water
- 1 tub whipped cream topping

Directions
1. In a small bowl, mix together peanut butter cookie crumbs and melted butter. Press the mixture into the bottom of the Ninja Multi-Purpose Pan or 8-inch baking dish.
2. In a medium bowl, use an electric hand mixer to combine the cream cheese, sugar, eggs, and peanut butter. Mix on medium speed for 5 minutes.
3. Place the chopped chocolate peanut butter cups evenly on top of crust in the pan. Pour the batter on top. Cover tightly with aluminum foil.
4. Place the water in the pot. Insert Reversible Rack into pot, making sure it is on the lower position. Place covered multipurpose pan onto rack. Assemble pressure lid, making sure the pressure release valve is in the SEAL position.
5. Select pressure and set to HI. Set time to 25 minutes. Press start/stop to begin.
6. When pressure cooking is complete, allow pressure to naturally release for 15 minutes. After 15 minutes, quick release remaining pressure by moving the pressure release valve to the vent position. Carefully remove lid when unit has finished releasing pressure.
7. Remove the pan and chill in the refrigerator for at least 3 hours or overnight before serving topped with whipped cream.

Per serving: Calories: 645 Fat: 47g, Carbs: 48g, Protein: 13g

Chocolate Peanut Butter and Jelly Puffs

These puffs are crunchy and full of nutrients. It is a perfect dessert or snack when going out.

Prep time 25 minutes/ Cook time 15 minutes/ Serves 4

Ingredients
- 1 tube prepared flaky biscuit dough
- milk chocolate bars
- Cooking spray
- 16 teaspoons creamy peanut butter
- 1 cup confectioners' sugar
- 1 tablespoon whole milk
- ¼ cup raspberry jam

Directions
1. Remove biscuits from tube. There is a natural width-wise separation in each biscuit. Gently peel each biscuit in half using this separation.
2. Break the chocolate into 16 small pieces.
3. Spray a baking sheet with cooking spray.
4. Using your hands, stretch a biscuit half until it is about 3-inches in diameter. Place a teaspoon of peanut butter in center of each biscuit half, then place piece of chocolate on top. Pull an edge of dough over the top of the chocolate and pinch together to seal. Continue pulling the dough over the top of the chocolate and pinching until the chocolate is completely covered. The dough is pliable, so gently form it into a ball with your hands. Place on the prepared baking sheet. Repeat this step with the remaining biscuit dough, peanut butter, and chocolate.
5. Place the baking sheet in the refrigerator for 5 minutes.
6. Place Cook & Crisp Basket in pot. Close crisping lid. Select AIR CRISP, set temperature to 360°F, and set time to 20 minutes. Select START/STOP to begin. Let preheat for 5 minutes.
7. Remove the biscuits from the refrigerator and spray the tops with cooking spray. Open lid and spray the basket with cooking spray. Place 5 biscuit balls in the basket. Close lid and cook for 5 minutes.
8. When cooking is complete, remove the biscuit balls from the basket. Repeat step 7 two more times with remaining biscuit balls.
9. Mix together the confectioners' sugar, milk, and jam in a small bowl to make a frosting.
10. When the cooked biscuit balls are cool enough to handle, dunk the top of each into the frosting. As frosting is beginning to set, garnish with any toppings desired, such as sprinkles, crushed toffee or candy, or mini marshmallows.

Per serving: Calories: 663, Fat: 25g, Carbs: 101g, Protein: 14g

CHAPTER 9: DRINKS 10 RECIPES

Nut Porridge

This is not a common porridge for many; however, when you try it you may not want to leave it again. You will love it.

Prep time 15 minutes/ Cook time 25 minutes/ Serves 4
Ingredients:
- 4 teaspoons coconut oil, melted
- 1 cup pecans, halved
- 2 cups of water
- 2 tablespoons stevia
- 1 cup cashew nuts, raw and unsalted

Directions:
1. Put the cashew nuts and pecans in the precision processor and pulse till they are in chunks.
2. Put this mixture into the pot of Ninja Foodi and stir in water, coconut oil and stevia.
3. Select sauté on Ninja Foodi and cook for 15 minutes.

Per serving: Calories 260, Fat 22.9 g, Carbs 12.7 g , Protein 5.6 g

Deliciously Traditional Clam Chowder

Need a chowder to cheer your day up? This is the perfect one for that purpose.

Prep time 6 minutes/ Cook time 17 minutes/ Serves 2
Ingredients:
- 2 6.5-oz cans chopped clams (reserve the clam juice)
- Water
- 2 slices bacon, chopped
- 1 ½ tbsp butter
- 1 onion, diced
- 1 stalks celery, diced
- 1 sprig fresh thyme
- 1 cloves garlic, pressed or finely minced
- ½ tsp kosher salt or more
- ¼ tsp pepper
- ½-lb potatoes, diced
- ½ tsp sugar
- ½ cup half and half
- Chopped chives, for garnish

Directions:
1. Drain the clam juice into a 2-cup measuring cup. Add enough water to make 2 cups of liquid. Set the clams and juice/water aside.

2. Press sauté button and cook bacon for 3 minutes until fat has rendered out of it, but not crispy.
3. Add the butter, onion, celery, and thyme. Cook for 5 minutes while frequently stirring.
4. Add the garlic, salt, and pepper. Cook for 1 minute, stirring frequently.
5. Add the potatoes, sugar (if using) and clam juice/water mixture and deglaze pot. Press stop.
6. Close Ninja Foodi, press pressure cook button, choose high settings, and set time to 4 minutes.
7. Once done cooking, do a natural release for 3 minutes and then do a quick release.
8. Mash the potatoes. Stir in half and half and the clams. Mix well.
9. Serve and enjoy garnished with chives.

Per serving: Calories 381; carbohydrates: 32.8g; protein: 29.3g; fat: 14.7

Vanilla Yogurt

Homemade yogurt always tastes great and with vanilla in the mix, the yogurt is so tasty and yummy.

Prep time 15 minutes/ Cook time 3 hours / Serves 2
Ingredients:
- ½ cup full-fat milk
- ¼ cup yogurt starter
- 1 cup heavy cream
- ½ tablespoon pure vanilla extract
- 2 scoops stevia

Directions:
1. Add milk, heavy cream, vanilla extract, and stevia in Ninja Foodi.
2. Let yogurt sit and press "slow cooker" and set the timer to 4 hours on "low."
3. Add yogurt starter in 1 cup of milk.
4. Return this mixture to the pot.
5. Close the lid and wrap the Ninja Foodi in small towels.
6. Let yogurt sit for about 9 hours.
7. Dish out, refrigerate and then serve.

Per serving: Calories 292, Fat 26.2 g , Carbs 8.2 g , Protein 5.2 g

White Cream Soup

This soup is a great way to make you feel good and restore your energy back and make your day.

Prep time 6 minutes/ Cook time 17 minutes/ Serves 2
Ingredients:
- ½ pounds stew meat
- 2 cups beef broth
- 1 ½ tablespoons Worcestershire sauce
- ½ teaspoon Italian seasoning
- 1 teaspoon onion powder
- 1 teaspoons garlic powder

- ¼ cup sour cream
- 3 ounces mushrooms, sliced
- Salt and pepper to taste
- 2 ounces short noodles, blanched

Directions:
1. Place the meat, broth, Worcestershire sauce, Italian seasoning, onion powder, garlic powder, sour cream, and mushrooms. Season with salt and pepper to taste.
2. Install pressure lid. Close Ninja Foodi, press the pressure button, choose high settings, and set time to 12 minutes.
3. Once done cooking, do a quick release. Open the lid and press the sauté button. Stir in the noodles and allow to simmer for 5 minutes.
4. Serve and enjoy.

Per serving: Calories 599; carbohydrates: 65g; protein: 39.6g; fat: 20.1g

Good-Day Pumpkin Puree

This is a refreshing dish that will fill you and leave you wanting more. It is a very easy to make dish that will make your work in the kitchen very easy.

Prep time 10 minutes/ Cook time 15 minutes/ Serves 2

Ingredients
- 2 pounds small sized pumpkin, halved and seeded
- ½ cup water
- Salt and pepper to taste

Directions
1. Add water to your Ninja Foodi, place steamer rack in the pot
2. Add pumpkin halves to the rack and lock lid, cook on HIGH pressure for 13-15 minutes
3. Once done, quick release pressure and let the pumpkin cool
4. Once done, scoop out flesh into a bowl
5. Blend using an immersion blender and season with salt and pepper
6. Serve and enjoy!

Per Serving: Calories: 112, Fat: 2g, Carbohydrates: 7g, Protein: 2g

Sweet Potato 'n Garbanzo Soup

What a better way to get your energy than this recipe? It will give you the energy you need for your body.

Prep time 7 minutes/ Cook time 10 minutes/ Serves 2

Ingredients:
- ½ yellow onion, chopped
- ½ tablespoon garlic, minced
- 1 can garbanzo beans, drained
- ½-pound sweet potatoes, peeled and chopped

- Salt and pepper to taste
- ½ teaspoon ground ginger
- ½ teaspoon ground cumin
- ½ teaspoon ground coriander
- ½ teaspoon ground cinnamon
- 2 cups vegetable broth
- 2 cups spinach, torn

Directions:
1. Place all ingredients in the Ninja Foodi except for the spinach.
2. Install pressure lid. Close Ninja Foodi, press the manual button, choose high settings, and set time to 10 minutes.
3. Once done cooking, do a quick release.
4. Open the lid and stir in the spinach. Press the sauté button and allow to simmer until the spinach wilts and serve.

Per serving: Calories 165; carbohydrates: 32.3g; protein: 6.3g; fat: 1.1g

Vanilla Pudding with Berries

This thick drink is so yummy, refreshing and filled with many nutrients. When it is chilled in a fridge for some time, it even becomes better.

Prep Time: 15 Mins, Cooking Time: 18 Mins, Servings: 4

Ingredients
- 1 cup Heavy Cream
- 4 Egg Yolks
- 4 tbsp Water + 1 ½ cups Water
- ½ cup Milk
- 1 tsp Vanilla
- ½ cup Sugar
- 4 Raspberries
- 4 Blueberries

Directions:
1. Turn on your Ninja Foodi and select Sear/Sauté mode on Medium. Add four tablespoons for water and the sugar. Stir it constantly until it dissolves. Press Stop. Add milk, heavy cream, and vanilla. Stir it with a whisk until evenly combined.
2. Crack the eggs into a bowl and add a tablespoon of the cream mixture. Whisk it and then very slowly add the remaining cream mixture while whisking.
3. Fit the reversible rack at the bottom of the pot, and pour one and a half cup of water in it. Pour the mixture into four ramekins and place them on the rack.
4. Close the lid of the pot, secure the pressure valve, and select Pressure mode on High Pressure for 4 minutes. Press Start/Stop.
5. Once the timer has gone off, do a quick pressure release, and open the lid.
6. With a napkin in hand, carefully remove the ramekins onto a flat surface. Let them cool for about 15 minutes and then refrigerate them for 6 hours.
7. After 6 hours, remove them from the refrigerator and garnish them with the raspberries and blueberries.
8. Enjoy immediately or refrigerate further until it is ready.

Per serving: Calories 183; Fat 12.9g; Carbs 12g; Protein 4g

Apple Pie Moonshine

In less than one hour you are able to make a very delicious Apple Pie Moonshine using Ninja Foodi at the comfort of your room.

Prep Time: 5 minutes/ Cook Time: 45 minutes/ Servings: 8 Ounces
Ingredients
- 16 Ounces Apple cider
- ¾ Cup White sugar
- 1 ½ Cup Caramel vodka
- 1 ½ Cup Everclear grain alcohol
- ½ Teaspoon Whole cloves
- 24 Ounces Apple juice
- 10 Cinnamon sticks
- ¾ Cup Brown sugar
- ½ Teaspoon Nutmeg

Directions:
1. Add apple cider and the apple juice into the pot of your Ninja Foodi.
2. Add, cinnamon sticks, white and brown sugar, nutmeg and whole cloves.
3. Select "sauté" on your Ninja Foodi and set 5 minutes.
4. After 5 minutes, close the lid and pressure cook for 45 minutes.
5. Allow about 15 minutes to release the pressure and open the lid so as to completely cool.
6. Add in the caramel vodka and Everclear and use a strainer to remove whole cloves and cinnamon sticks.
7. Serve and enjoy!

Per serving: Calories: 28/ Protein: 1g/ Fat: 1g/ Carbs: 5g

Chili-Quinoa 'n Black Bean Soup

This soup is very tasty and full of nutrients to keep you full of energy all day.

Prep time 6 minutes/ Cook time 20 minutes/ Serves 2
Ingredients:
- ½ bell pepper, diced
- 1 medium-sized sweet potatoes, peeled and diced
- ½ onion, diced
- 1 clove garlic, minced
- 1 stalk celery, chopped
- 1 1/3 cups vegetable broth
- 1 tablespoon tomato paste
- 1/3 cup diced tomatoes
- 1/3 can black beans, rinsed and drained
- 1 teaspoon each of paprika and cumin
- Salt to taste

- 2 tbsp quinoa
- 2 cups vegetable broth

Directions:
1. Place all ingredients in the Ninja Foodi. Give a good stir.
2. Install pressure lid.
3. Close Ninja Foodi, press the pressure button, choose high settings, and set time to 20 minutes.
4. Once done cooking, do a quick release.

Per serving: Calories 377; carbohydrates: 73.7g; protein: 18.1g; fat: 1.0g

Filling Cauli-Squash Chowder

The Cauli-Squash chowder is yummy, nutritious and a quick fix. You should try it today!

Prep time 5 minutes/ Cook time 12 minutes/ Serves 2

Ingredients:
- 1 tablespoon oil
- ½ onion, diced
- 1 clove garlic, minced
- ½-pound frozen cauliflower
- ½-pound frozen butternut squash
- 1 cup vegetable broth
- ½ teaspoon paprika
- ½ teaspoon dried thyme
- Salt and pepper to taste
- ¼ cup half-and-half

Directions:
1. Press the sauté button on the Ninja Foodi and heat oil.
2. Stir in the onions and garlic. Sauté until fragrant.
3. Add the rest of the ingredients.
4. Install pressure lid. Close Ninja Foodi, press the button, choose high settings, and set time to 10 minutes.
5. Once done cooking, do a quick release.
6. Open the lid and transfer the contents into a blender. Pulse until smooth. Serve with cheese on top if desired.

Per serving: Calories 103; carbohydrates:15.2 g; protein:1.9 g; fat: 3.8g

www.ingramcontent.com/pod-product-compliance
Lightning Source LLC
Chambersburg PA
CBHW081415080526
44589CB00016B/2547